Dr. Cooper's
Fabulous
Fructose Diet

Dr. Cooper's Fabulous Fructose Diet

by J. T. COOPER, M.D.
with Paul Hagan

M. EVANS AND COMPANY, INC. • *New York*

Library of Congress Cataloging in Publication Data

Cooper, James Thomas, 1935-
  Dr. Cooper's fabulous fructose diet.

  Bibliography: p.
  1. Reducing diets. 2. Fructose.
I. Hagan, Paul, joint author. II. Title.
III. Title: Fabulous fructose diet.
IV. Title: Fructose diet.
RM222.2.C615 613.2′5   78-27346
ISBN 0-87131-280-8

M. EVANS AND COMPANY, INC.
216 East 49 Street
New York, New York 10017

DESIGN BY DENNIS J. GRASTORF
Manufactured in the United States of America
9 8 7 6 5 4 3 2 1

To Paddington-Pooh, and all the other "Bears" in the Bariatric Society and to J. Daniel Palm, Ph.D., who started it all.

Contents

Introduction   9
1   Why Other Diets Fail   15
2   The Fail-Proof Diet   27
3   Five Ways to Become Fat-Free   37
4   Changing from Fat Thinking to
    Thin Thinking   83
5   Staying on the Diet   102
6   Staying Thin Forever   113
7   All Your Questions Answered   145
Appendixes   170
Bibliography   205
Index   209

Introduction

BY FOLLOWING the Fabulous Fructose Diet, people who have never been able to lose weight before have discovered that weight loss is easily within their grasp. The diet is based on my own experience and insight as well as on the cumulative research data of many hundreds of physicians and researchers. No discovery is ever made in a vacuum, and it is my hope that this system will be used as a starting point for still other advances in weight control.

The Fabulous Fructose Diet is based on my view that many dieters experience difficulty in handling glucose and that this difficulty leads to an inescapable and avalanching hunger. The result is a repeated inability to lose weight. Often the roots of these glucose problems lie in poor eating habits or in psychological quirks in which food is seen as the answer to all of one's problems. Whatever its origins, handling the glucose problem becomes an unbridgeable chasm that bars progress toward successful dieting.

On the Fabulous Fructose Diet program, described in detail in this book, thousands of patients have accomplished what to them was impossible: sustained weight control. Fructose is the key to this amazing diet. Fructose is a unique sugar that eliminates the glucose obstacle and helps one attain slimness in a natural, low-stress manner.

Many of my patients come to me only after attempting numerous other diets, after working with other physicians, after starving themselves in locked hospital wards, and after finally resigning themselves to being eternally overweight. By using the fructose diet they have successfully lost their unwanted weight, and they have sustained this loss. A 20- to 120-pound loss is equally easy using fructose. Whether you are an office worker, salesperson, housewife, or student you will find your problems anticipated and solved by the fructose method of dieting.

The fructose diet came about when I observed that many dieters were incapable of weight loss on any existing diet, even with great determination on their part and careful monitoring and support from doctor, family, and friends.

Early experience had already given me reason to mistrust the conventional wisdom in dieting via a "balanced, low-calorie diet." I am a former fatty myself and rose to the grand size of 240 pounds in 1967. The incongruity of a fat doctor attempting to counsel patients about any weight problems they might have hit me about the same time that I achieved my top weight. The advice of colleagues and friends to "push myself away from the table" was about as useful as a do-it-yourself brain surgery kit.

Embarking on a full-scale campaign to lose weight, I began to read everything I could get my hands on about diets. Textbooks, medical journals, and even old German research reports yielded little in the way of practical information. Gradually, though, I noticed that many diets had one thing in common—they were low in carbohydrates, however high they might be in controversial and even ridiculous fad foods. Many times an ingredient was added to a diet merely to make it attractive. These special foods ranged from alcohol, grapefruit, extra fats, extra roughage, honey, and oil, to other laughable things—laughable, that is, until one realized how desperate people were to find a good, workable diet.

My weight finally came off with the aid of a low-carbohydrate diet. Losing the weight produced an unexpected result. Word of success travels with the speed of light along the grapevine of the obese, and I soon had built up a practice of counseling and aiding obese persons.

In treating numerous overweight persons, I soon realized that some people simply could not stay on a diet because their energy levels were too low, a major drawback to low-carbohydrate diets. Fatigue dragged them down. And when they started to feel low and lifeless, they ate to make themselves feel better, to raise their energy levels. These people failed to stay on a diet not because they lacked will power but simply because their bodies had a physiological hunger that continually remained unsatisfied by almost any diet. There simply had to be a logical solution to their problem.

At this point I happened to read of some brilliant and exciting work by Dr. J. Daniel Palm on the use of fructose in human metabolism, particularly in relation to the stress response. Palm had discovered that the usual mechanisms for raising blood sugar could be short-circuited by changing, to fructose, the type of sugar consumed.

Unlike glucose, fructose does not require insulin in order to enter certain of the body's cells, so there is nothing to cause the feast-or-famine situation that has ruined so many dieters. (See explanation of the glucose-insulin trap in Chapter 1.) With fructose, there is only a smooth, low-keyed indirect flow of energy to the brain and the rest of the body. With the Fabulous Fructose Diet and other powerful systems like it, rapid, sustained weight loss is possible.

The Fabulous Fructose Diet, monitored by a competent physician, can permanently eliminate the problem of unwanted fat. With this book you can discover within yourself the slim person you have always wanted to be. You owe it to yourself to give it a try.

WHY FRUCTOSE DIETERS DO BETTER THAN THE AVERAGE DIETER DOES

There are two keys to my success in helping people take off weight. First is my weight sensitivity, which comes from being a formerly fat person. Even though I am now reasonably thin, I still think and act at times like a fat man. I still crave the same types of foods that were responsible for my weight gain. As a former fatty, I understand the struggle of fat persons to lose their excess weight.

Second is my unwillingness to demand from any person more than I feel he can deliver. An unrealistic goal set by a physician and then rigidly adhered to if the person has obvious handicaps can be a devastating blow to an already low self-esteem. It can contribute to diet failure. Many bariatric specialists feel that human behavior must be modified in small steps and that the emphatic support of the physician is particularly helpful. Learning to modify behavior is an important part of the FFD, one that will be discussed in Chapter 4.

Knowledge about dieting has improved dramatically in the last eleven years. Even with the newer diets, however, there have been a number of patients who have not been able to follow *any* of them. Failures occur despite careful monitoring, full motivation of the dieter, and intensive support. Many persons cannot stay on a diet for more than a few days at a time without feeling rotten, washed out, and discouraged. Halting their hunger is about as successful as stopping an avalanche in its path.

Fortunately for my patients and others around the country whose doctors my colleagues and I have trained, this no longer is the case. You don't have to feel rotten while you are dieting. You also don't have to feel washed out, weak, miserable, hungry, or like a target for the first temptation that comes your way. This is true whether you have 10 or 100 pounds to lose.

The breakthrough in dieting comes from a new knowledge of body chemistry and a reinterpretation of some well-established facts. Medical researchers now know why some people are unable to lose weight on conventional diets or why some people can lose weight, but regain it rapidly when not on a diet. As a result of some dramatic breakthroughs in the field of behavioral psychology, researchers also have the key to what motivates an obese person to overeat despite the knowledge that it is self-destructive.

I know what you need because I have been there. What I offer in this book is not a cure-all, a magic potion that works without any effort on your part, and above all, it is not another scientifically unsound program that could do more harm than good. The Fabulous Fructose Diet is safe when properly supervised by a physician. It eliminates the devastating effect of hunger that ruins so many diets, and it insures rapid weight loss, but it does require some effort on your part. With the help of this book, behavior that leads to overeating can be changed. And a maintenance diet shows you how to control your eating habits for the rest of your life.

1

Why Other Diets Fail

MOST OVERWEIGHT PERSONS have suffered repeated failures as dieters. You are probably familiar with the pattern. Often you lose weight and maintain a diet for anywhere from several days to several months, only to find that you regain the weight when you go off the diet. In addition, the time spent dieting is often pure agony, accompanied by depression, hunger, inertia, and an inevitable amount of self-contempt related to your inability to succeed at this one thing that means so much to you. You have undoubtedly experienced some of this yourself, or you would not be reading yet another diet book.

Until now—until the development of the fructose diet—modern science had not been able to produce a cure for overweight that eliminated the psychological and physiological barriers to successful dieting. The fructose diet is the first such breakthrough, for it appears to succeed in overcoming all the major drawbacks to dieting. In addition, it has a post-diet maintenance program that works. The best thing about the discovery of fructose as a diet aid is that it radically alters the lives of overweight people who have a problem with glucose tolerance, while it also works equally well for someone who is overweight and does not have a glucose-tolerance problem. The FFD works equally well for any overweight person, whether you need to lose 10 or 100 pounds.

SIGNS OF THE GLUCOSE-INSULIN TRAP

The fructose diet is based on the recognition of a pattern common to many dieters. This pattern might best be called the glucose-insulin trap. It is a hitherto inescapable factor in dieting that has wrecked thousands of diets.

Patients suffering from the glucose-insulin trap are, among other things, listless. They lack energy. Often an undercurrent of anger and self-contempt accompanies these physical symptoms. Years of research have shown that when given a glucose-tolerance test (GTT) many overweight persons display an abnormality in the way their bodies handle glucose. In one study done at the Hahnemann Medical School, Dr. Georgina Faludi demonstrated that over 80 percent of a group of significantly overweight persons had one or more abnormalities in their GTT curves, ranging from overt diabetes to reactive hypoglycemia. With so large a group showing abnormalities, the question often becomes not whether an overweight person has an abnormal curve, but how much deviation from the normal there will be.

Not only do problems in the ability to handle glucose occur with greater frequency in the obese, but these problems are often a major cause of diet failure, particularly when the problem—as is true with so many overweight persons—is tied to low blood sugar, or hypoglycemia. In Appendix 1, a technical examination of hypoglycemia and the four forms that it commonly takes in obese persons is presented; but for now it is enough to accept that hypoglycemia is one key to why so many problem eaters have until now been unable to diet successfully.

HOW THE GLUCOSE-INSULIN TRAP WORKS

To understand how dieters are trapped by their own glucose-insulin reactions, one need only look at how insulin and glucose interact in people with normal glucose reactions. Not surprisingly, the process begins with what you put into your mouth. A sizeable part of most people's diets consists of carbohydrates. Almost every carbohydrate is converted in the body into a simple sugar, glucose. Glucose enters the blood stream and travels throughout the body. While it does so, signals are set off that the glucose levels are rising. This sets off the release of insulin. Insulin is the hormone that assists the glucose in leaving the blood stream and entering most of the body's cells, where it is either stored as fat or used for energy. Insulin is responsible for lowering the levels of glucose in the blood. Normally, the elevation of the glucose level after eating, the secretion of insulin, and the resulting fall of glucose concentration in the blood is a smoothly and delicately balanced process.

The entire process happens within a couple of hours of eating.

In many overweight people, the process is slightly awry. For these unlucky souls an excess of insulin is secreted over and above the amount needed by the body to handle glucose adequately. Everything tends to happen in a slightly exaggerated way.

The insulin that is available tends to be used inefficiently, and there is often a delayed response on the part of the insulin to the rising blood-sugar levels. This slightly inefficient pattern results in the over- and undersecretion of insulin throughout the day. This, in turn, results in periods of elevated glucose levels, followed by periods of excessively low levels, or low blood sugar. During the periods of low blood sugar, an almost pathological urge to eat occurs. You eat, and the result, of course, is added and unwanted weight. This pattern repeats itself over and over again.

HOW INSULIN MAKES FAT

In addition to causing the low blood sugar that sets off eating binges, these peaks of insulin production have another bad effect. Insulin is much more active in stimulating fat production than it is in assisting glucose to enter the cells. Hyperinsulinism almost guarantees that a large part of the excess glucose will turn right into fat.

WHY YOU EAT DURING A
BLOOD-SUGAR CRISIS

Research has shown that the only way to avoid rapid ups-and-downs of glucose levels, with their accompanying insulin oversecretion, is to make sure that sugars of the type that stimulate insulin secretion are kept to a minimum. For most dieters in the past, this has meant learning to eat the more slowly digestible starches found in vegetables and fruits rather than the quickly digestible sugars such as candy bars, pastry, or other sugar-filled foods.

But simply eating fruits and vegetables and praying for results does not work for all dieters, largely because there is more to the entire process. Although insulin and glucose appear to be the villains, their inefficient utilization is really at fault. Without the surges of glucose and insulin, the body can pay attention to its normal routine and feed the brain and the rest of its parts without a crisis situation that alternates between feast and famine, which is what happens to those caught in the glucose-insulin trap just described.

But programmed into the body's nervous system is an instruction about the periods of low blood sugar. That instruction is that low blood sugar is a life-threatening event. You must eat to survive, according to your body's instructions. Short of locking someone in a room, there is no way to keep a person from eating once this order has been given. Every dieter needs to recognize that will power alone does not work when his body has gotten this message. Your body, not your mind, tells you to eat when you are caught in the glucose-insulin trap. (See Appendix 1.)

The way that the central nervous system signals the body during this crisis also produces some dramatic results, especially for dieters. When the glucose levels go way down, two messengers—glucagon and epinephrine—start to act on various sites in the body to stir up the production of glucose. This would be fine, except that epinephrine produces other reactions in the body. When released into the blood stream, it causes nervousness, the jitters, and irritability—all symptoms of low blood sugar and all symptoms that drive a person to eat. So, in addition to the purely biochemical reactions your body is undergoing, nervousness and irritability work on you; and most people in this state start to eat for relief. (Appendix 2 offers a more detailed explanation of this process.)

Constant fluctuations in the levels of glucose in the blood tend to set off minor or major surges of epinephrine all day long, and the result is a typically nervous, hyperactive, hungry, overweight person.

AVOIDING THE GLUCOSE-INSULIN TRAP

For years there has been no solution to this dilemma; no solution, that is, except for dieters to eat less and suffer mightily through the torture of physiological and psychological hunger.

Now there is an answer. It lies in the Fabulous Fructose Diet. The FFD is a nutritious, carefully planned, high-protein diet supplemented with fructose, a very special sugar that works to help take off weight quickly and safely.

Most exciting, though, is the victory fructose offers over the physiological and psychological aspects of dieting. First, it is a sugar; so, used as a diet supplement, it quells the craving for sweets. Second, fructose is absorbed slowly and directly by the small intestine, bypassing the usual biochemical channels that signal insulin to go to work to lower the glucose levels. Without excess insulin and the hypoglycemia that follows, there are no messengers such as glucagon and epinephrine. Without these messengers, there are no jitters. Finally, and incredibly, there is little or no hunger.

WHERE OTHER DIETS FAIL

Other diets have failed to take into account this hypoglycemic pattern. In turn, the key to healthy, no-hunger dieting is inaccessible until one looks in this direction. Other diet plans show you how to eat fewer calories or whatever the current fad is, but they do not prevent the torture of hunger that often accompanies such diets. And few obese people have the self-discipline to handle severe hunger pangs for very long. Then, too, when the abnormal or hypoglycemic curves are taken into consideration, one understands that a dieter's grouchiness or self-hate has a physical base. In a sense, these curves offer proof that your inability to stay on a diet is not entirely *psychological.* Your discomfort may have a physical base, which must be conquered and controlled before you can diet comfortably. The fructose diet, unlike most other diets, provides sound nutrition *and* controls hunger, thereby enabling you to stay on the diet until you have successfully taken off your excess weight.

WHO SHOULD NOT BE ON THE FFD

People with certain medical conditions should not be on any diet that is not carefully monitored by their doctor. In some instances, these people should not be on any diet at all. Do not go on the FFD or any other diet without medical monitoring particularly if you have liver problems, kidney problems, a history of gout, or diabetes. Insulin-dependent diabetics should not be on the diet at all, most are thin anyway and don't need to lose weight. Diabetics not on insulin have used the FFD under careful medical supervision, but this supervision is absolutely essential because of the complicated nutritional needs of diabetics. Children under the age of eighteen should not use this diet except with regular medical supervision.

Any woman who is or suspects that she may be pregnant should not begin the Fabulous Fructose Diet or any other diet, for that matter, without close medical supervision. Medical experts have long recognized that lowering the caloric or protein intake during pregnancy increases the risk of complications during childbirth and the chances of birth defects. If you are not sure whether or not you are pregnant, get a test before beginning the diet. Use adequate birth control measures during the diet. In fact, the first day of your period is an excellent time to begin the diet, as it usually offers assurance that you are not pregnant.

BE THIN FOREVER

I have stressed that weight loss can be maintained with the FFD. This is, in a way, the finest aspect of this diet. The experience of seeing people losing weight on other diets, then gaining it all back is indeed a sobering one. Most, if not all, of the people reading this book, have lost substantial amounts of weight at one time or another only to regain the excess pounds. The reason the weight comes back are interrelated. Unchanged eating habits, eating in response to external emotional stresses, and eating as a response to glucose-insulin stresses all pile on the pounds. Two of these causes of regained weight are eliminated immediately by the FFD.

The unchanged eating habits and the glucose-insulin stress will go first. The third cause, eating in response to external emotional stress, is built into the structure of a person's psyche. The feeling of success engendered by the FFD often carries over into other aspects of a dieter's life. Once you learn that you can control and change something as important as your eating habits, regaining control in other areas is often the next step.

If you follow the transition and maintenance programs exactly as laid out, there is no reason for you ever to be fat again. Using the Fabulous Fructose Diet, you can go to your target weight quickly and comfortably. You can learn a better, more satisfying eating pattern, learn to handle people your way, and learn to defuse emotional stress.

Failure is the sad result in traditonal programs that

attempt to provide a balanced diet and restricted calories and nothing else. The success rate in these programs is less than ten percent after a year. Many of them are well administered and based on sound nutritional thinking. There is just one problem. On such programs, people fail to lose, or if they have lost, they cannot maintain their losses. On the other hand, high-protein, low-carbohydrate regimes, backed up with assertiveness training and work on changing living habits and attitudes have been over 80 percent successful at the end of a year. Even though the FFD contains fructose, it is still considered a low-carbohydrate diet, and it has had a success rate of 90 percent after one year.

A new life with permanent weight loss awaits you. The Fabulous Fructose Diet can smash through your past failures and help propel you into that new life. The next chapter offers a number of detailed plans to take you where you want to go.

Five separate diet systems are provided in this book. The five systems are included so that a wide variety of life-styles, energy levels, and eating patterns can be accommodated. If you like to eat several small meals during the day, then the Meals-and-Munch Diet may be the answer for you. If you do strenuous work all day and only need to take off 20 or so pounds, then the slower Dependable Diet may be the best for you. Dieters seeking rapid weight loss will turn to the Basic Fructose Diet. The Vegetarian Fructose Diet is designed especially for vegetarians. The diet systems provide enough food to make you feel full all day; the fructose supplement satisfies your craving for sweets; and the pounds fall off rapidly.

While anyone beginning any diet is advised to see a doctor before starting, you can still handle this diet yourself. Two reasons to see a doctor, though, are to find out whether or not you have an abnormal glucose tolerance and to seek the doctor's counsel and support during the diet. Particularly if you are planning to stay on the diet for a long time—a perfectly safe thing to do—you will need the support and encouragement of someone such as your family doctor or even a bariatrician, a physician specializing in weight control.

HOW THIS BOOK CAN MAKE YOU A SUCCESSFUL DIETER

While most diet books describe the diet they espouse, the reader is generally left to his own devices once the diet has been explained. Not so with the Fabulous Fructose Diet book. Dieting is hard and a dieter needs to be given support every step of the way.

Chapter 2 of this book describes in detail the fructose diet and more about how it works. Chapter 3 contains all the information you need about the five diet systems and offers guidelines for choosing one diet over another. Chapter 4 shows how you can change your behavior to insure that you—and you alone—will be in control of your eating habits from now on. Chapter 5, unique among diet books, offers advice on sticking to the FFD when the going gets rough. Chapter 6 describes the Maintenance Diet.

And Chapter 7 answers all the questions that will undoubtedly accumulate as you read the book.

The easiest way to follow the diet is in its extrapolated form which appears at the end of Chapter 3. The best way of following it, however, is to read through the entire text of the book before turning to the insert.

WHY YOU WILL NOT FAIL

The Fabulous Fructose Diet has taken all the major problems of other diets and eliminated them. Whatever caused failure on other diets will not do so with this one. The Fabulous Fructose Diet was developed for the person who finds it impossible to lose. What works well for such a person is almost sinfully easy when only a moderate dieting problem exists. With this diet, there should be:

No calorie counting.

No decisions about what to eat.

No hunger.

No craving for food.

No feeling of being dragged out.

No meetings.

No waiting for days for a pound's loss.

No emotional downswings.

No kidding yourself that you can eat anything and
    still lose weight.

2

The Fail-Proof Diet

THE FABULOUS FRUCTOSE DIET is an entirely new type of diet system. Developed for problem eaters who have never been able to control their hunger, the diet has proved to be a dream system even for those who only need to drop ten pounds. Avoiding the insulin-glucose trap is apparently *the* key to successful dieting.

The Fabulous Fructose Diet has three main effects: (1) it eliminates the glucose-insulin trap, (2) it gives a rapid and safe weight loss, and (3) the majority of people on the diet suffer no true hunger.

Susan was a problem dieter who managed to lose hundreds of pounds on various diets, only to gradually regain most of them. Her combination of chocolate chip cookie binges and starvation diets were practically ruining her life. She was put on the FFD and an appointment with her doctor was scheduled for five days later. She was practically singing when she entered the doctor's office. "I feel like a human being, my brain can function, and my spirits simply woke up," she said. Now down to 118, she is using fructose in a permanent eating program to keep off the excess fat forever.

Lack of hunger is probably the major effect of the diet. Only a dieter who has lived through days in which every stray thought concerned food can appreciate a diet in which there is no hunger. Many overweight persons have a love-hate relationship with food. The thought of being denied access to food and the consequent hunger is terrifying to them. Rest assured that on this diet you will be eating as often as five or six times a day, and hunger will *not* be one of your problems. In fact, one of the problems many persons on the FFD report is managing to eat all the food required.

The no-hunger effect is produced in two ways. First, the fructose helps keep the brain supplied with enough energy to keep its alarm switch turned off. Second, when the fructose intake is between 30 and 60 grams a day, ketosis may occur to a very mild degree. Ketosis is a bodily process that occurs when there is a rapid breakdown of fats and carbohydrate intake is lower. The few ketone bodies that are occasionally formed during this process also play a role in suppressing hunger. They are not, however, numerous enough to produce all the problems usually encountered with the ultra-low-carbohydrate diets.

Another major effect of the FFD is the rapid weight loss. The Fabulous Fructose Diet has perhaps one of the most rapid weight-loss rate of any major weight-control program. An adequate amount of protein and other elements are included to make the diet safe and convenient to use, and the fat still goes almost as quickly as if nothing were eaten.

HOW MUCH CAN YOU EXPECT TO LOSE

Weight loss in the first week averages about ten pounds. This is common in any diet that restricts carbohydrates. Some of this loss is merely fluid loss. But a large amount—up to four pounds in a man and three-and-a-half pounds in a woman—is fat. And this is just the beginning! In the second week, the percentage of weight loss due to the elimination of excess water will slow down, and the loss of fat will make up a greater percentage of the total. On a sustained basis, fat loss averages around one-half pound daily on the Basic Fructose Diet. This adds up to 3½ pounds per week or 14 pounds a month of real fat loss.

Note the distinction between fat loss and weight loss. Scales, unfortunately, do not discriminate between the two. Weight loss that shows on a scale may mean less water, less protein tissue, or less fat in the body. Fat loss, however, is the name of the game. In fat loss, fat cells actually shrink. The only thing that will make them enlarge again is fat gained from improper eating. Water loss, on the other hand, is a temporary and sometimes not too desirable side effect, particularly when it is caused by diuretics. The water will usually come right back when the intake of salt or carbohydrates is resumed.

Actual weight loss will vary, too, from person to

person, depending upon an individual's basal metabolic requirements and levels of physical activity. Basal needs are the amount of energy necessary for the "housekeeping" chores of the body, such as heartbeat, breathing, digestion, and other basic functions necessary for life. Appendix 3 gives basal caloric needs for various heights and body sizes. Essentially, large, young, and tall males have the highest basal needs, while everyone else will tend to require fewer calories. A woman, by virtue of being smaller than a man, has fewer caloric needs. Small men have fewer caloric needs than do large men, and large women may have greater caloric needs than small men. This is just a fact of nature, and not much can be done about it.

A very important factor in weight loss is your activity level. A person working on a construction job and a person who does office work all day would have entirely different activity levels. The construction worker could probably eat more without gaining weight. Thus, if you elect to accompany the Fabulous Fructose Diet with an exercise program, you can expect to lose even more weight than these averages suggest.

THE IMPORTANCE OF PROTEIN

Protein loss, as a side effect of dieting, is a much more serious affair than is water loss. The vital organs, such as the heart and the liver, and the digestive tract and the muscles are not able to function if too much protein is lost. To add insult to injury, any massive weight loss caused by excessive protein loss is promptly replaced, along with lots and lots of fat, when the person resumes a regular diet. Weight loss due to protein loss is the worst of both worlds, it is unhealthy and it is doomed to fail as a weight reduction measure. Why does it fail? Because when protein stores are lost during a period of protein deprivation, a natural drive begins in the body to replace them. It begins with an uncontrollable hunger that forces the body to eat enough food to replace the lost protein. Along with the regained protein comes a substantial amount of fat. Thus the usual sequence of low-protein dieting is followed by excessive eating, which, in turn, is followed by a weight gain that often leads to even more pounds than before the diet was begun.

Everyone needs proteins to survive, although daily protein needs vary with the individual. Generally, most people need 50 to 75 grams daily. The amount necessary also varies with your sex, age, metabolic needs, and health. In addition, the kind of protein you consume is important. The best protein comes from eggs, fish, poultry, meat, lobster and other sea-food, soybeans, and milk-by-products. Protein can also be obtained from formulas in powder or liquid form, but protein in this form should only be taken under a doctor's supervision. Vegetables are also a source of protein, but you must make sure that an adequate amount of amino acids are contained in each day's ration. This is done by eating a variety of vegetables.

THE SWEET KEY TO SUCCESS
Fructose is not magic. It is, in fact, a diet supplement. Anywhere from 30 to 60 grams a day will

usually supply all the needs of the nervous system for energy. Any excess fructose consumed will simply be deposited as body fat or changed into dangerous "blood fat" or triglycerides. Excess fat in either place adds to the dangers of obesity, and extra blood fat in the form of triglycerides increases the likelihood of heart and blood-vessel disease.

Simply adding fructose to an ordinary diet, then, will not take off weight. In order to lose weight, you must go into a caloric-deficit situation. This is the only way to lose weight using fructose. Only if your body is fed less fuel than it uses will you lose weight.

Fructose is merely the raw material that will take the stress away from dieting and eliminate hunger. On the FFD, you will not crave food and your energy level will remain high. Fructose has been known for years to help increase the endurance and stamina of athletes. For example, the so-called wall that marathoners hit after topping the twenty-mile mark can be moved forward and sometimes eliminated entirely by taking adequate amounts of fructose prior to a race. In long races, there are no lows caused by excessive insulin since fructose does not stimulate insulin production as glucose does. Not only that, but fructose remains in the intestinal tract for a longer period of time than glucose does, trickling into the circulatory system and nourishing the body on an even basis. For the same reason that a long-distance runner who takes fructose need not suffer from insulin lows, a long-distance dieter need not either. Fructose is unique in that it nourishes the body without extracting a price in later misery, as glucose and sucrose do in so many persons.

A HEALTHY DIET

While on the fructose diet, carefully balanced amounts of protein, fructose, vitamins, and minerals * work to keep the body in an optimal condition to burn fat while safeguarding your energy and keeping your emotions on an even keel. This diet is also healthy in two other ways. First, it prevents the protein loss that occurs in many other diets. Second, it improves your overall health. The amount of cholesterol and trigly-cerides in the blood usually declines, helping to cut the risk of heart disease. Elevated blood pressure will usually decline and in many cases return to normal as the pounds drop off. Any excess of sugar in the blood generally declines. And best of all, the pounds vanish.

It is easier to be successful on the Fabulous Fruc-tose Diet than on other diets. And one success leads to another. Once you have taken off the first few pounds—thus proving to yourself that you can indeed do it—you will have an even easier time pushing yourself to take off the remaining weight. Your re-ward will be in watching the new, slim you take shape. Most diets promise weight loss without effort. The FFD promises to have eliminated almost all the effort.

* A complete vitamin and mineral supplement equal to or greater than the U.S. RDA for adults is recommended containing the 12 essential vitamins and 9 essential minerals.

THE FAILURE OF LOW-CARBOHYDRATE, HIGH-PROTEIN DIETS

In recent years, there has been a growing trend toward low-carbohydrate, high-protein diets. Yet these simply do not work for those battling low blood sugar and for many other would-be dieters. This is because low blood sugar is a stress like any other stress. It produces a normal response of an outpouring of cortisol from the adrenals to tell the liver to make more glucose. When the carbohydrate supply, the usual source of glucose, has been drastically reduced, the body starts to draw on protein for extra fuel. This constant demand on the adrenals, in response to repeated rounds of low blood sugar and combined with the external stresses of daily living, leaves the dieter with little or no "reserve" adrenal left.

Going on a low-carbohydrate, high-protein diet in such a stress state means that the needs of the brain for glucose fuel must be met by the liver, which normally works to convert amino acids to glucose, and that the liver must produce fuel from very few carbohydrates and protein. If you are already existing in a state of borderline exhaustion, however, the response to the need for more glucose fuel will be minimal, and the low levels of fuel will cause the brain to tell the body that it is tired and unable to continue. For many persons, this constant feeling of exhaustion and weakness for the entire length of time of a diet is an irresistible stimulus to eat, and the diet is quickly blown.

But by using fructose instead of protein as a source

of energy, the liver is effectively bypassed as a synthesizer. The adrenals don't have to put out the amount of cortisol they would otherwise be obligated to produce, and the exhaustion mechanism is short-circuited.

The fructose supplies the raw material for energy needs. On the FFD, then, there is no reason to feel weak or tired, with the possible exception of the first few days when your body and your psyche are adjusting to the diet. People on low-carbohydrate, high-protein diets often feel dragged out for the duration of the diet.

A FINAL WORD ABOUT HYPOGLYCEMIA

The mere mention of hypoglycemia produces a variety of reactions from the medical world today. Some doctors believe it plays a role in almost every ailment, and some doctors simply refuse to accept that such a condition even exists. Somewhere between the physicians who say that there is no such thing as hypoglycemia and their opposites who claim that it causes everything from African sleeping sickness to zebra skin dermatitis is the rational view, on which this book and the fructose diet are based.

The rational view and the fructose diet that emerged from it get results. People on this diet feel better than they have in years. They lose weight rapidly. With the help of the maintenance diet, they keep the weight off. Most important, they do not suffer any psychological trauma or hunger while dieting.

So regardless of whether or not hypoglycemia exists, if this set of symptoms appears to be common to a large number of people—in this case, overweight people—and if a certain conservative method of treatment—the fructose diet—helps control or elminate these symptoms, then it seems logical to pay attention to the symptoms and to use a treatment that eliminates them. This is why the fructose diet succeeds where so many other diets have failed.

3

Five Ways to Become Fat-Free

THIS CHAPTER contains all the information you need to choose and go on one of the five diet systems in the Fabulous Fructose Diet. All have been tested and have proven effective when used with the fructose supplement. The FFD systems offer safe, painless weight loss. The choice of the right system depends on you, your interests, and how active you are.

On any of these systems, you will be surprised at how quickly you will shed unwanted pounds—even if you have never been able to lose successfully before.

Before starting any of these diets, you should check with your doctor. Also, reread the section in Chapter 2 about who should not be on these diets.

The FFD systems are an extremely effective and powerful tool for weight loss; but, like any diet, they can be abused. On these diets you need to follow instructions exactly, eat everything on the diet, and drink the amount of liquid required each day.

Exercise is also an important tool for losing weight. Even a brisk, twenty-minute walk each day can result in an extra 100-calorie loss. More strenuous exercise results in still faster weight loss.

Read each of the diet systems carefully and decide which one best suits your habits and life-style. Choose one, follow it carefully, and you are on your way to becoming a lucky loser.

THE FABULOUS FRUCTOSE DIET SYSTEMS

The Fourteen-Day Priming Diet is designed for rapid weight loss for those who initially want to lose under 20 pounds. It is a good introduction to the Fabulous Fructose Diet systems and offers an opportunity for the dieter to go on a quick weight-loss diet before embarking on other diets in the system for even greater weight loss. It has the added bonus of a daily plan of suggested foods for those who want assistance in menu planning. Recipes for dishes may be found in Appendix 5 at the back of the book. The daily calorie deficit is about 1,000.

The Basic Fructose Diet is designed for rapid, sustained weight loss, while permitting the use of high-protein foods such as fish, seafood, chicken, veal, beef, pork, and lamb. The diet includes two large salads a day and regular small meals of sweet, delicious fructose. It should be used if you have a substantial amount of weight that you want to lose quickly. It is not suitable for you if you have an extremely variable living schedule, are preparing for athletic competition, or do heavy manual labor. The daily calorie deficit is about 1,500.

The Meals-and-Munch Diet works if you want a rapid weight loss but crave the taste of vegetables and fruits. This diet is higher in calories than is the Basic Fructose Diet, so weight loss is somewhat less rapid. It includes the smooth energy from fructose, and it allows more variety. This diet works best if you are fairly well disciplined, if you accept that when one apple a day is called for, it cannot be followed by a second or third. The daily calorie deficit is about 1,000 to 1,500.

The Dependable Diet is designed for those who have less weight to lose (under 20 pounds) or those who are in less of a hurry. It is well suited for a person who has noticed a steady upward creep of two to three pounds a year for several years. An athlete or someone with a very high activity level will find that the extra calories in this diet will keep energy levels high while the weight drops. The daily calorie deficit is from 500 to 1,000.

The Vegetarian Fructose Diet is a rapid weight-loss diet that uses meatlike substitutes for the meat units allowed in the Basic Fructose Diet. The diet includes fructose and salads. It is the one program that has been consistently successful for vegetarians. The caloric content can be adjusted upward (in consultation with a doctor) if you are an athlete or do heavy labor. The daily calorie deficit is about 1,000.

The Milkshake Diet. In addition to the five plans just described, there is a sixth program that can only be used with the aid of your doctor. It is called the Milkshake Diet and consists of premixed packets of protein and fructose that are combined with a liquid

and drunk. This formula is dispensed only by prescription through physicians who have taken a course
in its use. Weight loss is somewhat more rapid than
on the Basic Fructose Diet.

This is an excellent program for someone seeking
simplicity and rapid results, but it is not suitable for
anyone who does heavy labor. Discuss this diet with
your doctor if you are interested. For more information on the Milkshake Diet, see Appendix 4.

GENERAL GUIDELINES

A few general guidelines and suggestions apply to
all the diet systems. They are described on the following pages. Read these carefully before starting
any diet as they contain important, basic information.

Using Fructose

Fructose is the ingredient common to all these diets.
It is the most important part of the diet because of
its effect on the body's energy mechanism.

Fructose is available in health food stores, pharmacies, and some grocery stores. It can be purchased
in bulk, as a powder, in tablets, and in premeasured
packets, although it is exceedingly difficult to measure
powdered or granular fructose accurately without a
set of apothecary scales. For that reason, the tablets
and premeasured packets are recommended over the
powder form. The most economical tablets are of the
2-gram size. (Smaller tablets or tablets mixed with
protein are usually for those on an unlimited budget.)
At this writing, at least two companies produce pure
fructose in packets of slightly less than 3 grams each.

For those unfamiliar with the metric system, a gram is $\frac{1}{32}$ of an ounce. In this case, there is nothing to be concerned about, as the tablets and packets are all premeasured.

All that is necessary is to use any combination of tablets and packets that you please, so long as it adds up to the required amount. For instance, if 30 grams daily are needed, one could space ten 3-gram packets throughout the day, or one could have three 2-gram tablets with each of the three meals and three tablets with a sugar-free soft drink or decaffeinated coffee at 10 A.M. and again at 3 P.M. Fructose can be used to sweeten liquid drinks, can be sprinkled on food, or can be chewed as a tablet. It is the sweetest of all sugars and tastes delicious.

Checking Fructose Tolerance

It is advisable to check your personal tolerance for fructose before using it. Less than one percent of the population lacks the enzyme necessary to utilize fructose. These people will also generally become violently ill after eating a piece of fruit or anything made with table sugar (sucrose). They suffer from abdominal pain, vomiting, nausea, and low blood sugar after eating fructose or other sugars. Anyone with hereditary fructose intolerance obviously should not be on this diet. Rarely, some people who can eat table sugar still have a sensitivity to fructose, a lesser form of the intolerance just described. These persons react to fructose and other sugars with flushing, head-aches, dizziness, and weakness. The problem is not widespread, but you should test your tolerance by holding a little fructose under your tongue for two or three minutes. If you have no reaction, such as a headache, within five or ten minutes, you can begin taking fructose.

Fructose should also be introduced to your diet gradually. It is absorbed more slowly into the body, from the digestive tract, than are other types of sugars. While this is a great help in providing a smooth, even energy flow, it can cause occasional problems of mild diarrhea if 30–60 grams of fructose at one time are suddenly added to a restricted diet. To avoid this problem, begin with 10 or 15 grams, go to 25 the next day, then to the full 30 or whatever level of intake is prescribed for you. With delicious fructose to supply energy needs, you will be well on your way to successful dieting.

The fructose taken daily should be spaced out over the entire day. You may eat less fructose than is called for if you are not hungry unless a minimal intake is specified. The amount depends, to a great extent, on how much is needed to satisfy your craving for sweets. A good practice is to chew up two or three of the tablets about thirty minutes before a meal in order to take the edge off your hunger, or you may substitute a fructose-sweetened drink, such as lemonade, to achieve the same effect.

If you like lemonade, you will have no trouble at all consuming your daily ration of fructose. The various brands of sugar-free lemonade mixes, with no more than four calories per 8-ounce serving, lend themselves to being sweetened with fructose and can be used as the vehicle for all fructose intake.

Remember, the secret of using fructose is to spread it out in small portions over the entire day rather than gulping down the entire day's fructose in one portion.

A Word About Fats

Fat intake has been kept to a minimum, although there is some via the meats and vegetables on the FFD systems. On several of the systems, you are allowed a specified amount of butter, oil, or real mayonnaise per meal. Except where specified, though, do not eat any fats that are not part of the recommended foods on the diet.

Spices and Herbs

Any of the noncaloric spices and herbs are permitted on these diets, and they can, in fact, be used to enliven the food you eat. Salt in judicious amounts, pepper, horseradish (plain—not the sauces that often contain sugar), basil, dill, mint, cumin, and any other similar taste enhancers are permitted.

Beverages

You will spend a lot of time on this diet drinking fluids. This helps you lose weight by flushing excess water out of your tissues and keeps you healthy by giving all the burned fat and protein by-products an exit. On this diet, you should try to drink at least 80 fluid ounces a day. Lesser amounts can be drunk if this much fluid intake makes you uncomfortable. Drinks can be water, decaffeinated coffee, herb teas;

or clear, sugar-free soft drinks. Water is the preferred drink since it has no calories or additives.

Two cups per day of regular caffeinated coffee or tea are permitted, then decaffeinated coffee or diluted tea should be used as an alternative for the rest of the day. Check the label of any decaffeinated coffee to be sure of a low carbohydrate level.

Caffeine is kept down because it is an appetite stimulant. It is contained in both regular coffee, tea, and cola-type drinks that are colored brown. For that reason and to avoid sugar, the only soft drinks permitted are the light-colored, sugar-free drinks. Read the label to be sure they contain no caffeine.

Sugar-free sodas generally contain sodium. If you are drinking more than two a day, they can hold in excess water. For this reason, avoid making these your sole source of fluids. Do not overlook mineral or bottled waters, which contain no sugar, no calories, and have an interesting taste.

Artificial Sweeteners

The only sweeteners that do not contain sugar or other carbohydrates are saccharin tablets or liquid. *Do not use powdered artificial sweeteners*. Read the labels carefully before you use any sweetener. If the ingredients listed for these sweeteners include lactose, maltose, dextrose, dextrins, sorbitol, or xylitol, then you know that they are forbidden. One favorite tactic of some companies is to label them "a blend of nutritive and nonnutritive sweeteners." Avoid these sweeteners.

Vitamins and Minerals

One reason the Fabulous Fructose Diet is so safe and effective is the careful planning for all nutritional elements. To insure a balance of the necessary vitamins and minerals required each day, supplements are a necessary part of the diet. You can either take a one-a-day vitamin, along with potassium if ordered by your doctor or purchased in a health food store or pharmacy, or you can buy individual vitamins and minerals. Specific requirements are mentioned under the heading *Minerals and Vitamins* in each diet.

Cooking Methods

As much as possible, foods should be cooked without animal fat, butter, or oil. Use a commercial pan spray if you like. Protein foods should be baked, broiled, or panfried. Sauces, stuffings, breading, or batters are not allowed.

Meat, fish, and poultry shrink when they are cooked, and most of the amounts given in this book are for already cooked meat. About one-fourth of a food's weight is lost in cooking, so if 4 ounces of meat are called for, buy approximately 5 ounces.

Vegetables should be boiled, steamed, or baked and eaten without butter or sauce.

Forbidden Foods

Foods that are not allowed on any of the FFD systems include the following: alcohol in any form, beans, bread, candy (except for those in Appendix 5 and those made with fructose), cereal, all chewing gum and breath mints (even the so-called sugarless ones), corn, crackers, ice cream and ice milk, whole milk and all other forms of milk for drinking purposes, catsup, macaroni and other pastas, potatoes, and rice. Avoid all foods containing any form of sugar other than fructose. No type of coffee creamer, either powdered or liquid, is permitted.

A Word About Yogurt

Yogurt has in recent years been recognized as a diet food, yet it often does not qualify as that at all. The sour taste of this food often masks a large amount of sugar. The high-caloric frozen yogurt is mostly a cruel joke on dieters and is definitely forbidden; it usually has more calories than an equivalent amount of ice cream does.

Yogurt is allowed in some forms on this diet, and some of the recipes in Appendix 5 list it as an ingredient. When using yogurt for this diet, be sure to buy the unflavored, plain kind. Do not buy vanilla, as this is high in sugar and calories. Other flavored, premixed yogurts are also forbidden on this diet.

FOURTEEN-DAY PRIMING DIET

This fourteen-day diet can open up new vistas for you in the area of dieting, hunger control and weight loss. With the use of fructose and a controlled intake of high-quality protein foods it is now possible to lose weight without the torture of hunger and without the loss of energy and weakness that accompany less natural diets. This is one diet that actually demands that you take in all the foods and beverages specified, or the results will not be as good.

There are ample opportunities to substitute one

food for another with the diet if something does not appeal to you. The nice thing is that since everything is given in protein shares there are few calculations necessary. A one-share item can simply be swapped for another one-share dish and your protein intake and results remain the same. There has been a deliberate effort to get you interested in new foods and new ways of eating them. Sometimes a traditional breakfast has been specified. Try these new tastes and see how you like them. You may be surprised at how good they taste.

The Diet Plan
GENERAL INSTRUCTIONS

All weights given on the diet are cooked weights with the exception of clams and liver, which are weighed raw and then cooked. Numbers in parentheses give the number of shares in the dish or food. Any dish may be substituted for any other at any time, provided they have the same number of protein shares. Example, two ounces lean beef (1) can be substituted for two eggs (1) or any other one-share item.

All food must be either baked, broiled, boiled, steamed, or pan-fried with nonstick pans or with vegetable oil spray. Battering, stuffing, or similar calorie-adding cooking techniques are not to be used. When an asterisk (*) follows a dish name when first mentioned it means that a recipe for this dish is included in Appendix 5.

Code for meals: B-breakfast, MM-mid-morning, L-Lunch, MA-mid-afternoon, D-dinner, AD-after-dinner.

Day One

B. Coffee, hot tea, or hot herb tea with six grams (2 envelopes) granulated fructose. One scrambled egg (½) and two ounces lean grilled ham (1). Potassium gluconate (KG) tablet (595 or 599 milligrams size).

MM. One serving French Lemonade* or eight ounces sugar-free Kool-Aid-type powdered beverage with fructose added*.

L. Three-ounce lean, ground-beef patty, pan-fried and drained well (1½). Brush cooked surface lightly with 1 teaspoon Worcestershire or soy sauce. Salt and pepper to taste. Raw celery, green peppers and ½ dill pickle as relish dish. KG tablet. Tea or coffee with six grams granulated fructose added.

MA. Three of the two-gram fructose tablets (this is the most economical size) chewed or dissolved in mouth followed by large glass of water, diet soda, decaffeinated coffee or tea.

D. Crabmeat cocktail made with three ounces crabmeat (1) and flavored with the juice of one-half lemon or lime. Raw spinach salad with mushrooms and Orange Delight Salad Dressing*, 3 tablespoons. KG tablet. Each salad for this and all subsequent meals should fill an eight ounce measuring cup when packed loosely. Two ounces chicken livers (1) sauteed 5 to six minutes over moderate heat in nonstick fry pan with 1 ounce mushrooms, 1 teaspoon margarine and 1 teaspoon chopped

onions with one teaspoon sherry. Coffee, tea,
or hot herb tea with six grams fructose added.

AD. French Lemonade or sweetened Kool-Aid-type
beverage. Multiple vitamin.

A NOTE TO THE READER: To avoid repetition we
ask you to note that the potassium gluconate (KG)
tablet is always given with meals, three times a day.
The multiple vitamin (any good brand that has the
Recommended Daily Allowance of all vitamins and
minerals) is usually taken after dinner, but could be
taken at bedtime as well.

The permitted beverages are always given using
the schedule given above, but if your tastes don't require quite as much fructose with each drink, you
could use the excess fructose at some other time during the day, either in tablet form, or in syrup or
granules as desired.

Day Two

B. One poached or soft-boiled egg (½). Permitted
beverages.

MM. Permitted beverage.

L. Four ounces cod (2) baked in foil with thyme
and imitation butter flavoring. Garnish with
parsley and slice of lemon or lime. Tossed salad
with lettuce, cucumbers, green peppers and
raw mushrooms and diet Italian, French, or
Vinegar and Oil Salad Dressing*. Permitted
beverages.

MA. Three fructose tablets chewed or dissolved in
mouth with permitted beverages to follow.

D. Four ounces lean beef (2), broiled or pan-fried with permitted sauce (one teaspoon of either Worcestershire or soy sauce) brushed over meat after cooking. Spinach and mushroom salad with one boiled egg (½) cut up into salad. Use up to three tablespoons of diet-Italian or Orange Delight Dressing. Permitted beverages.

AD. Permitted beverage.

Day Three

B. Permitted beverages. Chicken Liver Omelet* (2).

MM. Permitted beverage.

L. One Tuna Crispie* patty (1). Permitted beverage. Head lettuce salad with vinegar and oil dressing, up to 3 tablespoons.

MA. Three fructose tablets with permitted beverages.

D. Four ounces light meat of turkey or chicken (2) either on the side, or diced and added to the evening salad of lettuce, cucumber, mushroom, celery and green pepper. Add up to three tablespoons of any of the diet dressings permitted. (See listing following in Appendix 5.) Permitted beverages.

AD. Permitted beverage.

Day Four

B. Permitted beverages. One wedge (1/6 portion of full recipe) of Paddington's Quiche* (2).

MM. Permitted beverage.

L. Four ounces pan-broiled veal (2). Cook over slow heat on non-stick surface. Add a small amount of garlic and/or lemon juice, or brush *lightly* with a small amount of melted butter with one teaspoon white wine. Tossed salad with three tablespoons permitted dressing. Permitted beverage.

MA. Three fructose tablets with permitted beverage.

D. Two and one-half ounces broiled salmon (1) with lemon slice. May be brushed with the Seafood Dip* mixture or served with the juice of ½ lemon and butter-flavored seasoning. Permitted beverage.

AD. Permitted beverage.

Day Five

B. One fried egg (½) served on top of a three-ounce ground beef patty (1½). Permitted beverages.

MM. Permitted beverage.

L. Three ounces baked haddock (1) cooked in foil with mushrooms, chopped green peppers, imitation butter flavoring and salt and pepper to taste. Tossed green salad with permitted dressing, 3 tablespoons. Permitted beverages.

MA. Three fructose tablets with permitted beverages.

D. Four ounces of lean beef, broiled and brushed

with permitted sauce (2). Cover with ¼ cup of mushrooms sauteed in 1 teaspoon margarine with 1 teaspoon sherry and the juices from the beef. Raw spinach salad with three tablespoons permitted dressings and a crumbled, well-cooked and drained bacon slice. Permitted beverages.

AD. Permitted beverage.

Day Six

B. Two eggs (1), fried or scrambled. Serve with two ounces lean pork (1), pan-fried and well drained. Permitted beverages.

MM. Permitted beverage.

L. Two ounces beef liver (1), lightly cooked over medium heat in 1 teaspoon oil with two slices onion (1½ tablespoons). Add 1 teaspoon sherry with the oil if desired. Cook for about six minutes. Endive salad with three tablespoons permitted salad dressing. Permitted beverage.

MA. Three fructose tablets with permitted beverages.

D. Four ounces baked chicken breast (2). Remove skin and fat prior to weighing. Season with imitation butter flavoring, salt and pepper. Brush with permitted sauce. Tossed green salad with three tablespoons permitted dressing. Permitted beverages.

AD. Permitted beverage.

Day Seven

B. Paddington's Quiche, 1 wedge (2). Permitted beverages.

MM. Permitted beverage.

L. Three ounces sirloin of beef, brushed with permitted sauce (1) and served with a Spring Garden Salad*. Permitted beverages.

MA. Three fructose tablets served with permitted beverages.

D. Five ounces scallops* (2) cooked as directed. Use Seafood Dip instead of usual sauces. Head lettuce salad with three tablespoons permitted dressing. Permitted beverages.

AD. Permitted beverage.

Day Eight

B. Four ounces lean beef (2), broiled and brushed with permitted sauce. Permitted beverage.

MM. Permitted beverage.

L. One Tuna Crispie pattie (1) served on a bed of endive lettuce with ½ lemon and a spring garden salad. Permitted beverages.

MA. Three fructose tablets with permitted beverage.

D. Flounder-Fromage Fillet*, four-ounce serving (2) with lemon slices for garnish. Spinach and mushroom salad with 1 slice crisp bacon crumbled into salad and three tablespoons permitted salad dressing. Permitted beverage.

AD. Permitted beverage.

Day Nine

B. Two scrambled eggs (1) with permitted beverages.

MM. Permitted beverage.

L. Ten ounces raw or steamed clams (2) or a three-ounce ground beef patty with one slice American cheese melted over it (2). One-half lemon permitted along with clams or 2 teaspoons mustard with ground beef. (Permitted sauce can also be used to brush on beef.) Tossed green salad with three tablespoons permitted dressing. Permitted beverage.

MA. Three fructose tablets along with permitted beverage.

D. Stuffed Green Pepper* with four ounces ground beef (2). Permitted beverages. Endive salad with Vinaigrette Salad Dressing*, three tablespoons.

AD. Permitted beverage.

Day Ten

B. Two fried or scrambled eggs (1) with two ounces lean ham (1). Permitted beverages.

MM. Permitted beverage.

L. Four ounces lean veal (2), cooked exactly like lunch for Day Four. Permitted beverages. Tossed salad with three tablespoons permitted dressing.

MA. Three fructose tablets with permitted beverages.

D. Two ounces lean pork pan-broiled and brushed with permitted sauce (1). Large bowl of raw salad as relish. Serve with juice of ½ lemon or lime. Cut celery, peppers, lettuce, etc. into small wedges or cubes and munch. Permitted beverage.

AD. Permitted beverage.

Day Eleven

B. One wedge Paddington's Quiche (with ham) (2) plus permitted beverages.

MM. Permitted beverage.

L. Four ounces lean broiled beef (2), cut into strips and stir-fried with two teaspoons oil, ½ cup bean sprouts, one tablespoon diced onions, two tablespoons chopped green peppers, plus salt and pepper to taste. Stir in pan until meat and vegetables are browned on all sides. Serve with one teaspoon soy sauce. One tossed salad with three tablespoons permitted diet dressing. Permitted beverages.

MA. Three tablets fructose along with permitted beverages.

D. One Salmon or Tuna Crispie patty (1) and permitted beverages. Spinach and mushroom salad with three tablespoons permitted salad dressing.

AD. Permitted beverage.

Day Twelve

B.   Butterworth Omelet* (2) plus permitted beverages.

MM.   Permitted beverage.

L.   Four ounces Stuffed Flank Steak* (2) with Spring Garden Salad and three tablespoons permitted salad dressing. Permitted beverage.

MA.   Three tablets fructose along with permitted beverage.

D.   Two ounces sliced light meat of chicken or turkey (1). Tossed green salad with three tablespoons permitted dressing. Permitted beverage.

AD.   Permitted beverage.

Day Thirteen

B.   One egg (½) with two ounces lean pork or ham (1). Permitted beverage.

MM.   Permitted beverage.

L.   Three ounces crabmeat (1) as cocktail or two ounces boiled shrimp (1), with either juice of ½ lemon or 1 teaspoon soy sauce. Serve on lettuce. Two ounces diced lean ham (1) and one chopped boiled egg (½), both to be added to a tossed green salad with three tablespoons permitted salad dressing. Permitted beverage.

MA.   Three fructose tablets along with permitted beverage.

D.   Two ounces cod (1), cooked as on Day Two,

Lunch. Tossed green salad with three tablespoons permitted dressing. Permitted beverage.
AD. Permitted beverage.

Day Fourteen

B.   Three ounces cooked lean ground beef (1½)
topped with one poached egg (½). Place one
slice American (½) or Swiss (½) cheese over
top, melt in oven and serve with salt, pepper,
mustard or other permitted sauces. Permitted
beverage.
MM. Permitted beverage.
L.   Two ounces halibut (1), cooked in foil with
salt, pepper, imitation butter flavoring, and
slice of lemon. Permitted beverage. Raw spinach and mushroom salad with one slice crisp
bacon crumbled into salad and with three
tablespoons permitted diet salad dressing.
MA. Three fructose tablets along with permitted
beverages.
D.   Three ounces chicken livers, sauteed as on Day
One, dinner meal (1½). Endive salad with
three tablespoons permitted salad dressing.
Permitted beverages.
AD. Permitted beverage.

PERMITTED SALAD MATERIALS

Each salad consists of about one loosely-packed
measuring cup in size and should contain only lettuce,
endive, raw spinach, celery, escarole, leeks, pimento,
green peppers, cucumbers, mushrooms, bean sprouts,

and dill pickles. Salads are added to give variety and roughage to the diet.

PERMITTED LIQUIDS

Up to two cups of regular coffee each day, the rest should be decaffeinated. Up to two cans of diet soda daily, preferably without caffeine. (Caffeine tends to trigger excess hunger in many people.) All the water, weak tea, herb tea and mineral water you desire. You may have as many as two servings of French Lemonade a day, or the alternative fructose-sweetened Kool-Aid-like drink. Both are listed in the recipe section. It is desirable, but not mandatory, that your fluid intake be high. Best results will be obtained on a high intake of all types of fluids.

SEASONINGS

Any spice may be used in moderation, along with the juice of one lemon or lime, one teaspoon of mayonnaise, margarine or butter.

PERMITTED SAUCE

One teaspoon of either Worcestershire sauce or soy sauce daily.

SUPPLEMENTS

A multiple vitamin-mineral tablet with the U.S. Recommended Daily Allowance for an adult is taken once daily. In order to help prevent some of the fluid retention often seen on rapid reducing diets we also take one potassium gluconate (KG) tablet three times a day with each meal. The strength is usually 595 or 599 milligrams per tablet.

A WORD ABOUT EGGS

It is up to the patient and the doctor as to whether or not eggs are consumed. It has been my experience that few people are ever harmed by the short-term use of the amount of eggs specified on this diet. If you do not wish to use eggs, there are ample substitutions of equivalent amounts of protein in other dishes that will get the same results for you.

RESTRICTIONS

The only restrictions are to avoid sugar (except for fructose), alcohol, and excess caffeine. Any of these could trigger excessive hunger and make you go off your diet. IF IT IS NOT ON THE DIET SHEET, YOU CAN'T HAVE IT!

FRUCTOSE

The diet works mostly because of the addition of fructose in several forms and because of the elimination of the triad that usually triggers abnormal hunger (Alcohol, caffeine and sugars other than fructose). Leaving off the fructose will destroy part of the effectiveness of the diet and make you more vulnerable to hunger. For this reason, you MUST take all of the fructose every day you are on this diet.

The three forms of fructose that are economical are the two-gram chewable tablet, the three-gram packet and the new 90% fructose syrup, sometimes called

Fructose90. The tablets do not dissolve in liquids and must be chewed or dissolved in the mouth, followed by liquids. The packets come in boxes of 50 and are used to dissolve in hot or cold liquids. The Fructose90 syrup is best used in cooking and in liquids, with each level teaspoon containing six grams of fructose and a small amount of other carbohydrates. *Never* use bulk granulated fructose as it is too easy to use too much.

THE BASIC FRUCTOSE DIET

This is the most powerful weapon in the war on fat. On this system, you should lose at least one-third to one-half pound of fat a day. Many persons will experience initial losses of up to 10 pounds in the first week. This will be largely water loss, but you can usually count on at least 2½ to 3½ pounds of fat loss per week with even moderate activity. For this diet to work well you must follow the directions exactly. Thousands of people have used it to lose weight easily and safely, *when* they followed directions. Making up your own rules not only will not speed weight loss, but may well cause the diet to fail.

The Diet Plan

Generally, this diet requires the fructose supplement of 30 to 40 grams per day; a large amount of protein foods such as fish, poultry, and meat; two large salads; potassium and other minerals and vitamins; and lots of liquid. That's all there is to the diet. The protein keeps you healthy; the fructose gives you energy; and the potassium and other minerals and vitamins keep the wheels oiled.

Under a doctor's supervision, you can stay on this diet for months, losing 50, 75, or 150 pounds—whatever is needed. This diet does require effort and will power, but you will find that it is much easier to manage than any diet you have tried before.

FRUCTOSE

Take 30 grams per day to begin with. This is obtained by using fifteen 2-gram tablets or ten 3-gram packets mixed with drinks or food with your meals or a combination of tablets and packets totaling 30 grams daily intake or more as determined by your physician.

PROTEIN

First look at Table 3–1 and find the number of protein shares for your height and sex.

Everyone on the diet gets at least five protein shares a day. These can be eaten in any order during the day. For example, one possible pattern would be one share for breakfast, two for lunch, and two for dinner. Or you might follow the same pattern, but save one of the dinner shares for a midevening snack with some fructose. Use a pattern that fits your hunger urges and life-style, but you must eat at least three meals a day. Between-meal nibbling is one of the habits you are trying to banish from your life.

Larger individuals will have higher protein needs and need more than five protein shares. Table 3–1 shows that a man six feet four inches tall will need eight protein shares per day. You can still divide this quantity into a three-meal pattern. In this case, an acceptable pattern might be two shares for breakfast, one at 10 A.M., two more for lunch, two for dinner, and one later in the evening. A pattern that is guaranteed to wreck a diet is to save all the protein and fructose and eat one giant meal in the evening. This type of pattern would create ravenous hunger, nausea, and probable diet failure.

Table 3–2 shows the amount of food (cooked weight, unless otherwise specified) that make up one share. You will need a scale that gives accurate weights in ounces. Estimates are inaccurate and will result in slower weight loss. Many dieters prepare large portions of different types of protein food, cut them into one-share sizes, and store them in the refrigerator. When a meal is needed, they simply pull out a portion and reheat. The protein shares can also be mixed with the salad foods, or eaten as a cold buffet with lemon juice for flavoring.

TABLE 3–1.
Calculation of Daily Protein Shares

To determine how many protein shares you will require each day, find your height to the nearest two inches. If your height is between two of the figures, go to the next higher. A person with a height of five feet seven inches would use the figures for five feet eight inches. Protein shares are given on the basis of ideal weight rather than actual weight. The protein requirements are listed in the next column and given to the nearest gram. The last column is the proper number of protein shares to consume each day.

WOMEN

Height (Inches)	Ideal Weight Pound (Kilograms)		Daily Protein Requirement (Grams)	Number of Shares
4' 10"	102	(46.4)	70	5
5' 0"	107	(48.6)	73	5
5' 2"	113	(51.4)	77	5
5' 4"	120	(54.6)	82	6
5' 6"	128	(58.2)	87	6
5' 8"	136	(61.8)	93	6
5' 10"	144	(65.5)	98	7
6' 0"	152	(69.1)	104	7

MEN

5' 2"	123	(55.9)	84	6
5' 4"	130	(59.1)	89	6
5' 6"	137	(61.8)	93	6
5' 8"	145	(65.9)	99	7
5' 10"	153	(69.6)	104	7
6' 0"	162	(73.6)	110	7
6' 2"	171	(77.7)	117	8
6' 4"	181	(82.3)	123	8

NOTE: Men under five feet take five shares daily. Those above five feet, but less than five feet two inches take six shares. Women under four feet ten inches still take five shares. Women over six feet take a maximum of seven shares. Each share equals approximately 15 grams of protein with a varying amount of fat, depending on the grade and cut of the protein source.

SOURCE: Health and Welfare Canada. Reproduced by permission of the Minister of Supply and Services Canada.

TABLE 3–2.

List of Servings Equaling One Protein Share

Type of Protein	Ounces Equal to One Share
Clams, raw	5.0
Cod	2.0
Crabmeat, canned or fresh, steamed	3.0
Eggs (boiled, poached, scrambled or fried without fat)	2 eggs
Haddock	2.7
Halibut	2.0
Flounder	1.7
Lobster	2.9
Shrimp, drained	2.2
Scallops	2.2
Tuna, water-packed	3.0
Salmon, Atlantic, canned	2.4
Salmon, broiled	2.2
Beef, lean (choice or good)	2.0
Beef, ground (10 percent fat)	2.0
Beef, sirloin	2.5
Beef liver	2.0
Chicken, light meat, skinless	1.6
Chicken, dark meat, skinless	1.8
Chicken liver	2.0
Lamb	1.6
Pork, lean loin roast	1.8
Ham, lean	2.0
Turkey, light meat, skinless	1.6
Turkey, dark meat, skinless	1.8
Veal, lean, loin cut	2.0

NOTE: Weights are cooked weight except for clams and liver, which are weighed prior to cooking. Weights are rounded off to 1/10 ounce and should be adhered to as closely as possible. Amounts are slightly different than those on the Fabulous Fourteen-Day Fructose Diet.

SOURCE: U.S. Department of Agriculture, Handbook No. 456.

SALADS

Salads are a part of the diet that creative cooks really enjoy. They are also the part of the diet that offers the greatest chance for variety. Included in the Basic Fructose Diet are two large salads per day, each equaling about one cup of loosely packed ingredients. Permitted foods include lettuce, endive, raw spinach, celery, escarole, leeks, pimento, green peppers, cucumbers, raw mushrooms, and dill pickles. (Sweet pickles are not permitted.) Salads are included to add variety and roughage to the diet. Not eating them will not affect the diet, although you will experience fewer bowel movements.

SALAD DRESSING AND FATS

The only homemade dressing permitted is made from one teaspoon of safflower oil, and up to one tablespoon of vinegar or lemon juice per salad. You can also use bouillon if you can find a sugar-free variety. Safflower oil can be obtained from health food or grocery stores. It is recommended because it contains a very high percentage of linoleic acid, an essential dietary component. If you live in a rural area and cannot obtain safflower oil, you may substitute corn or peanut oil. Calories add up quickly with oil, so remember the proportions—one teaspoon of oil and one tablespoon of vinegar.

There are also some commercial dressings suitable for use with the diet. Read the labels carefully, however, because if a dressing says "diet" or "low calorie" on the label, this does not necessarily mean it is suitable for the FFD. As a general guideline, any commercially prepared salad dressing that has no more than six calories per tablespoon of dressing is acceptable.

No fats such as mayonnaise or butter are allowed in this diet system.

MINERALS AND VITAMINS

The FFD acts as a natural diuretic. All of the excess fluid normally held in the tissues, making you feel bloated and fat, is lost. There is a small loss of potassium and sodium on the diet due to the lack of fruits and the decreased amount of green vegetables eaten. These minerals can easily be replaced by the use of a potassium supplement.

The most economical form of potassium is prescription, but many times you can find comparable bargains at health food stores. Potassium is measured in milliequivalents as a standard way of determining potency. Twenty milliequivalents of potassium chloride, potassium gluconate, potassium citrate, potassium bicarbonate, or any other potassium salt are each equally potent, even though the total weight of each compound may be different.

Persons on diuretics and certain other medications that can cause potassium loss may need more supplemental potassium and should consult their doctor for the exact amount. Others, particularly those who are taking over 40 grams of fructose daily, will have little or no ketosis and will only need the usual amount they would receive in fruits and vegetables usually consumed when not reducing. Health food stores sell potencies of potassium (usually the gluconate) of no more than two to two-and-a-half milliequivalents per tablet. The four to six tablets daily will do many things, including helping your energy and fluid balance problems. Think of them as part of your dietary intake and not just as "more pills" to take.

Since you are going to have a checkup with your doctor before going on this diet (or any other), it pays to have him check your mineral levels, particularly the sodium and potassium. If he feels that you need more than 10 to 15 milliequivalents of potassium he will order more. He may use a liquid, powder, effervescent tablet, or regular compressed tablet by prescription.

All potassium can potentially cause irritation of the intestinal tract, and may have a less than delicious taste. You may want your doctor to let you try samples of several brands to find one that is most palatable to you. The least objectionable form seems to be the potassium bicarbonate tablet (6.47 milliequivalents). Taking the potassium with food is usually a good way to insure that irritation is minimal or absent.

Just as the basic diet, by its design, is deficient in potassium, it is also rather low in calcium and magnesium. This is the reason for the extra minerals as listed below and also the reason for the extra folic acid. The folic acid is normally found in green vegetables, but these are minimal on this diet.

One way to supply other nutrients is to take an all-purpose vitamin each day. Choose any commercial preparation that meets the recommended daily allowance (RDA) of vitamins and minerals.

The following supplements are suggested in addition to potassium:

1. Multiple vitamin-mineral tablet (as discussed above), all RDA amounts included, daily.
2. Calcium tablet: one to three daily.
3. Magnesium gluconate, 500 milligrams, one or two daily.
4. Folic acid, 0.1 milligrams one daily.
5. A B-50 formula with 50 milligrams of every B-complex factor present, one daily. This may sound excessive, but experience has shown that it definitely benefits those on low-calorie reducing diets.
6. Extra B-6, usually 50 milligrams, one or two a day, whenever there is excessive bloating. This is certainly necessary for women taking any form of birth control pill or female hormone supplement, and is also indicated in cyclic edema related to the menstrual cycle. B-complex supplements are available in most stores that carry vitamins. They are not essential to the program, but they do contribute to its high success rate.

A word about salt—common table salt contains sodium, an essential mineral. Unless your doctor forbids it, you are allowed a moderate amount of salt on the FFD. Do not go overboard, but do use it if desired.

This, then, is the Basic Fructose Diet. It is beautifully simple: fructose, protein, water, potassium and other minerals and vitamins, five elements that move you rapidly along the road to permanent weight loss.

Most other systems in the Fabulous Fructose Diet draw on these sections, and you will be referring back to them.

When and What to Eat

Spread your protein intake over the day, usually into three meals. Spread out the salad and fructose meals, too. Notice when hunger develops during the day and save a good portion of the fructose for about an hour before these times.

One of my patients had an almost constant pattern of being hungry at 4 P.M. every day. Dinner was not until after 6 P.M., which left her vulnerable for two hours. A cup of decaffeinated coffee with nine grams of fructose at 3 P.M. solved the problem and kept her on her diet.

Another patient worked at a construction job and had little time for frequent feedings. When lunch rolled around, he was starving and vulnerable to the lunch wagon's junk food. It was impossible for him to resist these temptations until he began using chewable fructose tablets. One or two tablets every hour with a little water were all he needed to keep from being hungry. He is now a slim and healthy worker with fewer sick days and a lower blood pressure.

On the FFD, take all the proteins—you will need them. One of the most common and deadly traps of any low-calorie diet is the tendency to feel that if eating so much protein helps, then eating half as much will help even more. This is an unhealthy view of dieting that can result in discomfort, protein or other dietary deficiencies, and inability to stay on the diet. Eating less than the allowed amount of protein actually slows down the fat loss, while the body's protein is being broken down for energy. Always take as much as recommended, never more or less.

The same guideline applies to water. On this kind of diet, your kidneys are your best friends. Waste products must be eliminated, and, except for a few items eliminated by the liver via the intestines, the kidneys do all the work. A large intake of fluids, particularly water, insures that the urine does not become too concentrated and that there is enough volume and flow through the kidney-filtering tubes to remove waste products.

THE MEALS-AND-MUNCH DIET

For many, the prospect of going on a high protein and fructose diet for weeks or even months, without letup, is a little more than they can stand. The Meals-and-Munch Diet is a solution. Weight loss is a little less rapid, but this diet has more variety and is less strict than the Basic Fructose Diet. It also has the same smooth energy flow and low hunger level as the others.

The Diet Plan

Essentially, the Basic Fructose Diet is followed for three days of the week, usually Monday, Wednesday, and Friday. And the following diet is adhered to on Tuesday, Thursday, and Saturday:

Breakfast

Two boiled or poached eggs, or 2 ounces lean meat, or one-half cup cottage cheese. All the permitted calorie-free beverages desired.

Lunch

One portion of a List 2 vegetable. (Vegetable lists follow.)

Four ounces, cooked weight, of lean fish or seafood, beef, or poultry, cooked as described for Basic Fructose Diet.

One piece or portion of fresh fruit. (Apple, orange, pear, peach, apricot, half grapefruit, one-fourth cantaloupe, or one-half cup strawberries.) No canned, frozen, or dried fruits, no raisins, and no juices are permitted.

A raw salad with ingredients from List 1 vegetables only. Eat all you want, with any of the dressings described with the Basic Fructose Diet.

Dinner

Same as lunch but omit the fruit. If desired, you may omit the fruit for lunch and have it with this meal instead.

On Sunday only two meals are eaten: brunch and dinner.

Brunch

Three-egg omelet with 1 ounce of ham chunks, peppers, mushrooms, if desired, *or* 4 ounces (cooked weight) of lean beef, fish, or poultry, *or* three boiled eggs with 2 ounces hard cheese or 4 ounces cottage cheese.

Dinner

Six ounces (cooked weight) lean beef, fish, or poultry.

One piece or portion of fresh fruit, as described earlier.

One portion of a List 2 vegetable.

One portion of a List 3 vegetable.

FRUCTOSE

On the days when you follow the Basic Fructose Diet, use the amount of fructose recommended, usually 30 to 40 grams. On the Meals-and-Munch days, take 30 to 40 grams of fructose, spread out over the day. On Sunday, take only between 20 and 30 grams for the entire day.

SALADS

Salad foods are drawn from List 1 vegetables. These foods must be eaten raw, and they can be eaten in unlimited quantities.

SALAD DRESSINGS AND FAT

The low-caloric salad dressings described in the Basic Fructose Diet are allowed here. You can also make a dressing, using one teaspoon of oil and vinegar or lemon juice to taste. Up to one teaspoon of fat —butter or oil—is permitted per day on this diet in addition to that used with the salad dressing.

VEGETABLES

LIST 1 VEGETABLES

Use these to make salads and for snacks.

Cabbage	Peppers, red and green
Cauliflower	Radishes
Celery	Sauerkraut
Cucumbers	Spinach
Lettuce	Tomatoes
Mushrooms	

LIST 2 VEGETABLES

The cooked vegetables in this category have a higher caloric value than those in List 1 Vegetables, primarily because the List 1 Vegetables are mostly composed of cellulose when raw; when cooked, the food is converted to simple carbohydrates, which are more readily digestible and which contain more available calories. They may be cooked by baking, steaming, or boiling, the same methods used to cook any of the vegetables on this diet system. One portion equals one loosely packed measuring cup.

Asparagus	Mushrooms
Broccoli	Mustard greens
Brussels sprouts	Spinach
Cabbage	String beans
Cauliflower	Tomatoes
Collards	Turnip greens
Eggplant	

LIST 3 VEGETABLES

These vegetables contain the highest calories of all. Beware of eating too much of these vegetables, either in cooked or raw form, and eat them only once a week. Fresh, frozen, or canned vegetables may be used. One portion equals one-half measuring cup.

Carrots	Rutabaga
Green peas	Yellow squash
Pumpkin	Zucchini

MINERALS AND VITAMINS

A one-a-day vitamin is recommended on the Meals-and-Munch Diet. The same vitamin and mineral supplements recommended for use on the Basic Fructose Diet are also highly recommended for this diet.

THE DEPENDABLE DIET

This diet is for those who wish to lose a small amount of weight or who want a more leisurely diet pace. This diet is also good for those persons who do relatively heavy physical labor and do not want to cut their caloric intake very much.

The Diet Plan

FRUCTOSE
The daily intake of fructose is initially set at a level of 40 grams. It may be in tablet or packet form or in one of the desserts permitted on this diet, made with fructose. Recipes for desserts made with fructose are in Appendix 5.

PROTEIN
You are allowed three to five servings per day (usually three, unless you are very active). Each serving of protein consists of 4 ounces, cooked weight, of *lean* beef, lamb chops, ground beef, or veal. Food with fillers, such as cold cuts, sausages, frankfurters (even the all-meat ones), or meatballs is not permitted. Pork is permitted occasionally, but is too high in fat content to be used often. Poultry is permitted if the skin and fat are removed before cooking. This includes chicken, turkey, duck, Rock Cornish hen, and capon. Either bake, broil, boil, or panfry foods without oil or butter, stuffing, breading, or batter.

Fish and shellfish may be used, also in 4-ounce portions. Most lean fish and crab, lobster, or shrimp may be eaten. Cooking methods are the same as for meat and poultry. Once or twice a week, you may have a 5-ounce portion of chicken, beef, or pork liver, precooked weight. If you cook with onions, they count as your vegetable for the day.

Cheese is permitted, but it can be a dieter's trap. You can consume much more than is desirable. If you want cheese, consider 1 or 2 ounces as a serving, and never eat more than one serving a day. One-fourth cup of cottage cheese is also considered one serving. It provides needed calcium. Cottage cheese or ricotta cheese, 1 ounce being a serving of the latter, are also permitted in certain pastry recipes. (See Appendix 5.) You may have as much as two of these servings a day, either plain or combined with other food.

Eggs are an excellent source of protein and can be boiled, fried, scrambled, poached, or in omelets. Remember to use a nonstick pan spray instead of butter or oil when cooking. As a general guideline, do not eat more than two eggs per day on this diet.

By taking in as many as five servings and no less than three of the protein foods listed, you can satisfy your body's need for protein and keep your health and strength while the fat is coming off.

SALADS
Eat the same portion size and number of salads as on the Meals-and-Munch system. Again, the roughage is important. The same dressings as for the other systems are allowed.

SALAD DRESSINGS AND FATS
The salad dressing permitted is the same as the Basic Fructose Diet dressing: one teaspoon oil and one tablespoon vinegar or lemon juice to taste. Also, on this diet, one teaspoon of fat—butter, mayonnaise,

or oil—is permitted per meal in addition to the oil in the salad dressing.

VEGETABLES

Vegetables allowed are artichokes, asparagus, bamboo shoots, broccoli, brussels sprouts, cabbage, cauliflower, chard, Chinese cabbage, crookneck or yellow squash, eggplant, kale, kohlrabi, mushrooms, okra, peppers, sauerkraut, spinach, string beans, tomatoes, water chestnuts, and zucchini squash. You may have unlimited amounts of any of these as long as they are raw, but no more than one-half cup of any one of them per day in the cooked form. Feel free to eat lots of the raw vegetables because their extra bulk has a filling effect and also contributes to bowel regularity.

MINERALS AND VITAMINS

In this system, potassium needs are partly met by the food intake, and the calcium needs are also partly covered by the intake of fermented milk products. About 10 milliequivalents of potassium are needed daily from prescription sources or over-the-counter preparations. Your doctor may have to adjust the potassium requirement to your individual needs. Three or more tablets daily of calcium is the usual amount for this diet. You may want to take vitamin C and vitamin B-6 as dietary supplements.

DESSERTS

On the Dependable Diet, desserts are allowed. They include D-Zerta Gelatin but not D-Zerta Pudding, which has too many of the wrong type of carbohydrates. One piece of Cooper's cannoli or Cooper's cheesecake (recipes are in Appendix 5) is permitted every three to four days.

If you are very active and walk over thirty minutes a day, you can probably get away with one of the fructose-containing desserts every other day.

SUPPLIES
Appendix 6 contains information on buying fructose and foods containing fructose.

THE VEGETARIAN FRUCTOSE DIET
Before this diet, when a vegetarian needed help in losing weight, only a so-called "balanced vegetarian diet" could be offered. The usual result was no weight loss. Frequently, vegetarian dieters became quite discouraged and quit. Now there is a solution. The hunger-destroying powers of fructose and meatlike vegetarian substitutes are united in the Vegetarian Fructose Diet, which has worked successfully for many vegetarians.

The Diet Plan
FRUCTOSE
The fructose content of this diet starts at 30 grams daily and is raised in 10-gram units about every three to four days, up to 60 grams, until there is absolutely no abnormal hunger or craving.

VEGETABLE PROTEIN UNITS
Each unit listed in the table below contains from 9.5 to 16 grams of protein and from 60 to 225 calories

per unit. Companies other than the two listed also produce vegetarian meatlike products, but only these two have furnished their calories and protein contents. The lists were obtained from Dr. Wilmer Asher of Denver, Colorado, and adapted from his book, *The Rapid Weight Reduction (RWR) Program.*

Each day select and eat five of the units from the vegetarian food list. They may be baked, broiled, boiled, or panfried without oil or butter. Do not bread or batter any foods and avoid all sauces except lemon. Also, eat no more than two servings of the same food in a day. Your daily calorie intake will normally be about 700 to 800. With this amount of food intake, weight loss should exceed 2 pounds a week. For the average patient, no more and no less than five units of protein per day are needed. The only exception might be someone on a special diet or a very active and tall person who requires more because of his occupation. For these special cases, consult with your physician to determine a larger intake. Anything not mentioned in the food list is forbidden.

SALADS
Two large raw salads are permitted each day with the standard dressing of one teaspoon oil, one tablespoon of vinegar and lemon juice to taste.

MINERALS AND VITAMINS
Follow the same daily mineral and vitamin suggestions as for the Basic Fructose Diet: 10 to 15 milliequivalents of potassium, magnesium gluconate, folic

acid, a multiple vitamin and plenty of B vitamins, and up to three calcium tablets a day.

VEGETARIAN FOOD LISTS

Although we have tried to avoid the mention of brand names in the main section of the book except where absolutely necessary, on the Vegetarian Fructose Diet, the foods are so specific that brand names are essential. Two separate lists of products are given, however, to avoid any suggestion of endorsement. These products are also widely available throughout the U.S.

TABLE 3–3.
Vegetarian Food List
LOMA LINDA FOODS

Name	Calories	Grams of Protein	Grams of Carbohydrates
(each counts as one protein unit)			
2 Big Franks	172	15.9	4.8
Dinner Bits (5 bits)	115	11.7	3.0
Dinner Cuts (2 cuts)	90	14.9	3.9
2 Linketts	153	14.9	1.8
Meatlike Loaves (Beef Loaf ¼-inch slice)	120	10.9	2.8
Chicken Loaf (¼-inch slice)	114	10.9	1.7
Turkey Loaf (¼-inch slice)	125	11.3	2.8
Luncheon Loaf (¼-inch slice)	122	11.1	2.8
Proteena (½-inch slice)	141	15.8	4.1
Rediburger (½-inch slice)	153	14.2	3.9
2 Tastee Cuts	84	15.0	2.9
Vegeburger (¼ cup)	63	10.6	2.3
Vegeburger (NSA ¼ cup)	66	10.6	3.0
2 Vegechee (½-inch slice)	212	16.6	3.6
Vegelona (¼-inch slice)	77	9.9	2.6

WORTHINGTON FOODS

Name	Calories	Grams of Protein	Grams of Carbohydrates
(each counts as one protein unit)			
Stripple Zips (1 oz.)	130	14.0	2.9
Worthington Vegetarian Burger (⅓ cup)	100	12.0	3.4
2 Chaplets	100	16.0	4.0
4 Saucetts Links	160	13.2	2.0
2 Vegetable Scallops	60	10.0	1.8
Soyameat Beeflike (1½ oz.)	75	9.5	3.2
Soyameat Fried Chickenlike (3 pieces)	195	13.5	1.5
Vegetable Steaks (2 pieces)	60	11.6	.8
3 Veja Links	225	12.3	3.6
Wham (3 oz.)	135	12.6	3.9
2 Beeflike Slices Frozen Roll (2 oz.)	110 (frozen)	12.0	2.8
Chickenlike Slices, Roll (2 oz.)	150 (frozen)	12.0	1.6
Chic-ketts (2 oz.)	110 (frozen)	14.0	2.2
Wham, 2 slices	110 (frozen)	12.0	2.4

4

Changing from Fat Thinking to Thin Thinking

No one comes into this world fat. In fact, most obesity results from years of learning a particular pattern of dealing with food, exercise, and even work and other personal habits that contribute to that big, bad habit—eating too much. Somewhere along the way, you learned to eat more than your body burns in fuel each day.

Although most of this book has been devoted to relearning your actual eating patterns through diet, and you have by now probably realized that dieting without excessive hunger is possible, the chances are that your dieting will never be truly successful unless you also examine the behavior that motivates your eating addiction. You need to learn to change your behavior, particularly how that behavior relates to what you put in your mouth.

This may sound like a big task until you realize

and accept that all these patterns were learned and that what is learned can be unlearned.

Just think about this for a minute: eating habits and what is considered proper to eat does not come from Above. They are learned from family, friends, acquaintances, books, television. Realizing that there is nothing sacred, fixed, or immutable about the types and amounts of foods you eat is the first step toward changing your eating habits. An American may dream about chocolate cake, while a Greek craves baklava, and a Soviet Georgian longs for fresh, homemade yogurt. These are all learned behaviors, and all are subject to change. The Soviet Georgian gets just as much pleasure from his low-fat, low-calorie yogurt as Americans do from their high-fat, high-calorie chocolate cake.

Furthermore, dietary habits are changing every day in response to new products coming on the market and to changing prices. One key to dieting is to recognize this and then to learn to plan menus that respond to your new interests and needs.

GETTING WHAT YOU WANT FROM LIFE

Many overweight persons live with a tremendous undercurrent of anger and resentment. They dislike events in their lives or the way people treat them, and in frustration or resentment they turn to eating. Food is one of the world's greatest tranquilizers and rewards, and after a few hundred repetitions of using food to reward yourself, your reaction to food becomes automatic. When angry, frustrated, depressed, or nervous, you eat.

Rather than try to change a behavior pattern that is so deeply imprinted on your mind, the first step is to avoid being maneuvered into situations that make you angry, nervous, depressed, or frustrated. Today, there are an entire group of techniques for doing this, all gathered under the general heading of *assertiveness*. Many persons misunderstand the nature of assertiveness. Being assertive does not mean that you become aggressive or combative.

It simply means that you work out your relationships with other people so that they suit your needs, because, after all, you are the only person who is accountable for what happens in your life. *Your* life is the one that is being shortened by overweight, and *your* peace of mind is shattered when you let someone push you into overeating. Being assertive rests on a basic belief that you are a worthwhile person, valuable to yourself and to others. Many people are so busy deriding themselves that they never do see their own abilities and worth. Yet, constantly assuming that you are no good and that you can do nothing right only gives you the satisfaction of saying "I told you so" when your negativism causes you to fail. This is a very bleak way to look at the rest of your life.

Tuning in to your inner worth is easy, but it requires constant effort. You might want to begin with some background reading. *How to Be Your Own Best Friend* by Newman and Berkowitz (Random House, 1974) and *When I Say No, I Feel Guilty* by Manuel J. Smith (Dial Press, 1975) offer good explanations of assertiveness. Both are available in paperback and at most libraries. Courses in assertiveness are frequently given by church groups, the YMCA, colleges, and counseling centers. Reasonably priced, they are well worth taking.

The central thought in all assertiveness training is that only you are the judge of your life and actions. We all begin life as dependent children who must please adults to get what we want. As adults, we must take the next step in growth and realize that it is now ourselves that we must please. This does not mean being negative, selfish, self-centered, and capricious. It means learning to express our feelings and desires in a positive and nondestructive mannner. No one gets everything he or she wants, but everyone can usually get what he or she needs.

For example, imagine that you have gone to a friend's home where you are offered a piece of cake. You decline, and she insists. If you relate to your friend in a childlike manner, you give in because you are afraid that she will disapprove or not like you anymore. Or you may try to manipulate your friend by saying that you really should not eat the cake since you are on a diet. This puts the burden of guilt on your friend. Or you might let someone else take responsibility by saying that your doctor won't let you have the cake.

Adult behavior, however, is to simply say no in a firm but pleasant manner and to continue to say no until the cake is no longer offered. This is called the parrot technique. No matter what is said, you continue to say, "No thank you, I don't care for any." (The parrot technique is particularly good for saying no to any proposition, including unwanted food and door-to-door salesmen, particularly those selling candies, cookies, and doughnuts in charity drives.)

Part of solving your own problems is learning that you cannot solve the problems of everyone else. One mother found that she was being manipulated into working for so many community organizations that she never had any time for herself or her family. All of her interlocking commitments made her nervous and resentful, and she ate out of frustration. Only when she learned to say no and started declining things that were not that important to her personally did she begin to get her weight under control. The organizations did not collapse without her, nor did her friends turn on her when she set up a schedule that was more workable and more fun for her.

Solving your own problems also involves dropping your attempts to manipulate other people into doing what you want. Tell the other person what you want them to do directly. Don't try to control someone by making him feel guilty or inadequate. For example, a wife is tired of sitting at home with the kids and wants to spend an evening out with her husband. She might begin by asking him if they could go to the movies the next night. He replies, "I'm tired, and we saw a movie last week." She agrees, but still sticks to her assertion, "Yes, you do work hard, but I would still like to go out." He is still not enthusiastic and comments, "You are really a movie freak." She stays with her point and offers a compromise, "Yes, I really do like the movies. Why don't we make it the day after tomorrow, and you can pick the movie."

He probably will agree at that time and figure that

a movie is not such a bad idea after all. There are a number of specific techniques that can be learned, including prompting another person, avoiding defensive responses, and offering a compromise. Some people seem to master these communications skills instinctively, but in most of us they are not fully utilized.

Avoiding emotional upsets by being assertive is more effective than any other single thing you can do about weight loss. Think about handling demands on you in terms of what is important to you, not to other people.

CHANGING YOUR EATING HABITS

Persons who are obese are extremely responsive to environmental cues to eat. The time of day, a certain location at home or work, watching television, an ad for potato chips, the sight or smell of food, all these serve as switches that turn on problem eating behavior. Everyone is bombarded by hundreds of such food cues during the day, but only a few of them, such as lunchtime and the thought that one has not eaten since breakfast, actually control when and what one eats if one is not obese. Fat people are not so lucky. Through habit and training, the cue to eat has become very closely linked to an irresistible urge to eat. Having will power and a firm resolve not to overeat is all well and good, but more often than not, habit conquers will power almost every time. A much more profitable course of action is to analyze your behavior and find out what causes you to eat. Then rearrange your life so you can avoid or minimize that particular cue.

Since self-knowledge is the starting point for change, the first step will be to track down and analyze your food habits. Begin to do this by keeping a simple food diary. Get a small pocket notepad and carry it with you constantly for a week. Do this before you begin to diet. Without trying to change what you normally eat, write down in precise terms (for example, 3 ounces of cheese and two oatmeal cookies) everything you eat or drink that has any calories at all, the time and place you ate it, how hungry you felt, and what made you want to eat or drink it. Boredom, nerves, or hunger are the kinds of responses you will probably note in the latter category.

Keep this record for a week and do not forget to include everything you eat, no matter how trivial. Often the act of writing a food down will diminish the amount of unconscious or automatic eating that you do. After a week, go back through the diary and look for your problem areas. Do you tend to be a night eater? Do you have trouble passing a delicatessen? Do you have an unconscious habit of nibbling while watching television? When do you overeat? Are certain types of food particular problems? Is it only with a certain friend or relative that you have trouble staying on a diet?

One teacher found that he fixed an evening meal, then drifted back into the kitchen about 7:30 P.M. for another snack, or two, or three. Once he recognized his problem, he learned to plan evening walks and other activities away from the kitchen. He now grades papers far away from the kitchen door, which is tightly closed after dinner. He also saves some of his fructose and a protein snack and eats them in his bedroom near bedtime.

Another dieter found that 3 ounces of meat would mysteriously grow into a pound or more as a mealtime portion. She solved this problem by asking a friend to help her cook and weigh out portions in advance and freeze them. She found that even the most powerful food cue could not push her to consume a piece of frozen meat.

If you find that the morning coffee break is doing in your waistline, plan a way around it. Bring an apple, a fructose drink, or fructose tablets with you. Take a walk around the block, work at your desk, or have a talk with a friend far away from the coffee room. Do whatever it takes to avoid walking defenseless into a room filled with junk food at break time. This is a prime example of overcoming the habits of years by rearranging *your* schedule. You are in control.

After you have eliminated the obvious problem areas, it is time to work on the areas that are providing subconscious signals. First, examine where and how you eat. The easiest way to keep track of it is with a list. Then try some of these suggestions for breaking your old eating habits.

1. Do all of your eating in one room, preferably the dining room, if you have one.
2. Always fully set the table with silverware and china before eating anything, even a forbidden

candy bar or a snack. Use a distinctive place mat if possible.

3. Put the fork down between bits and thoroughly chew one mouthful before taking another one. Some dieters have found that chewing each bite at least twenty times before swallowing and taking another mouthful helps. Many obese persons hurry through a meal in ten miuntes or less, yet about twenty minutes are required for the body to transmit the message to the brain that the stomach is full. In that time, an overweight person can consume a huge amount of food.

4. Fill the plates in the kitchen, and put only one serving on a plate. It is a good idea to cook only enough for one serving per person so there is little likelihood of leftovers.

5. Plan a pause of two to three minutes midway during the meal. As you develop more experience, actually walk out of the room for five minutes or longer, just to show yourself that you have developed self-control, then come back and finish your meal. Try to break the cycle that begins with food being set in front of you and ends when you have consumed the entire amount in conveyor-belt fashion.

6. Clear any leftover food directly off the plates into the garbage or disposal. This is particularly important in the mornings when many housewives or other persons who work at home are left alone with breakfast leftovers. They proceed to act as human disposals for any toast, bacon,

or rolls that are left over by the family. Clearing the table stops this.

7. To test yourself, set aside a portion of your favorite food at each meal. (This is to be used only on the maintenance plan. On other diets, you will need to consume the entire amount of food budgeted each day.) Allow it to remain uneaten and then discard it.

OTHER HELPFUL HINTS

Eliminate distractions that may cause you to start eating. High school taught most of us that it is hard to concentrate on studying if the radio or television is on and the phone is ringing. The effect is the same if you attempt to concentrate on reading or talking when everything reminds you of food.

Before beginning the diet, fatproof your house by throwing out or giving away anything that resembles a munchie. This is difficult if you live in a house with cookie addicts, or if there is only one person in the family who needs to reduce. But remember, junk food and desserts do not improve anyone's health, and most families are able to devise a way for nondieters to go out for their sweets while the dieter stays home, away from temptation.

Food shopping should be done only on a full stomach and while armed with a list. Take only enough money to buy what is on the list and leave the children at home. It is hard to resist a child who begs for junk food (when you are in a store full of nosy little old ladies who cannot imagine what you are depriving that child of). Even if you go alone to the store with a list, you must still fight all the resources of modern technology, which range from music and lighting to packaging and display, all trying to make you an impulse buyer. Be aware of their game and stick to your plan to only buy wholesome and economical foods.

Remember that boredom, anger, loneliness, and fatigue often lead to episodes of unthinking, automatic eating. Plan your day with the idea of avoiding these triggers. Have a list of pleasurable activities for the time when you might be bored or lonely. Movies, phone calls or letters to friends, a hobby, business tasks, shopping trips, visits to museums, new books to read, even purposely planned errands, all help. When you feel angry, remember what you have learned about assertiveness and try to change the situation. Anger will probably cost you more in emotional turmoil and possible eating binges than it is worth. Express your feelings, but do not go into an emotional orgy of hostility.

When shopping or out socially, avoid food shops and restaurants. Sit by a fountain rather than hanging over the counter of a pastry shop. You will be constantly bombarded by food stimuli wherever you go, so don't make it any more difficult than absolutely necessary.

If you gorge yourself every time you go to a church social, buffet, or any other social function, don't go. There are few functions so crucial they cannot be missed. Instead, use the occasion to have a party yourself. Get a group together and go bowling, skating, or walking. Use your imagination. If it is absolutely essential that you go, show up after you have had a full meal or bring a small plate of food for yourself, as well as a few sugar-free drinks if you are unsure of local supplies. You can leave the beverages in your car and go back outside for them if no permissible drinks are available. Never put yourself at the mercy of your host or hostess, because some of them have no mercy where dieters are concerned. If you must attend a dinner party, call ahead and ask for help in coordinating your meals. Most of your hosts will understand if they are really your friends. You might find that many of them have been in a similar situation themselves and are very accommodating.

Any social situation with alcoholic drinks is also a signal to eat. Avoid places with chips, peanuts, and other munchies on the bar and tables. Have a sugar-free drink, mineral water, or club soda. A bar can be a very tempting place for forbidden calories. Instead of taking a few drinks, try to arrange a walk after work to unwind or arrange to meet friends somewhere other than in a bar or restaurant. You don't have to be a hermit; simply use some imagination about where to go for recreation and relaxation. The change can be quite pleasant.

Learn to control the size of your food portions by having a standard-sized serving. You might even make a plate with an outline of a 4-ounce serving on it. Anything that does not fit into the circle is trimmed off and discarded. This is good training until you become experienced at the art of estimating sizes of portions. When in doubt, measure or weigh any food before you eat it.

THINK YOURSELF THIN

Mental attitude guides many of our daily actions. You have a mental image of yourself, and generally, you tend only to do things that fit with that mental picture. Clara, a dieter on the FFD, wanted to return to school to dig into English and history. She was, however, a 35-year-old mother of two, and being a student did not fit into the way she saw her world. As she practiced imagining herself slim, buying new clothes, horseback riding, having fashionable and low-calorie lunches, she realized that only her self-image was keeping her out of school. She began by seeing herself studying, buying books, registering for courses, sitting in class—and then she did it. Once she had worked her new self-image through in her mind, the reality became easy.

The same thing that Clara did to rethink her self-image works when applied to eating habits. You can, in a sense, imagine yourself thin. Follow these simple guidelines:

1. Picture yourself as a thin person. Visualize yourself in a mirror. Look at the way you will walk and move. In other words, design a concrete, detailed picture of yourself at your target weight, and spend a few minutes each day thinking about the new you.

2. Imagine yourself buying all kinds of clothes you can only wear if you are thin. See yourself in the store picking out small sizes, horizontal stripes, and huge plaids.

3. Imagine your refrigerator stocked—like a mod-

el's—with fresh eggs, fish, the makings for salad, and cottage cheese.

4. When someone offers you the wrong food, see yourself as you plan to be. Let the slim you stand beside the real you and help you say no to the offer.

The system behind many of the self-help books, such as Norman Vincent Peale's *Power of Positive Thinking* or Napoleon Hill's *Think and Grow Rich*, is founded on the power of imagery. Psychologists have recognized that it is very difficult to think of yourself in one way and act in another. Over a period of time, your thoughts and behavior tend to merge. For instance, an obese person may be constantly on a diet, but in his head, where the real action is, he is constantly eating some type of favorite, forbidden food. Unless that image is changed, he will tend to act as he sees himself—and out the window goes the diet.

To understand just how strong a mental image is, tests have shown that even after losing weight, formerly obese people give wide berth to obstacles such as chairs or door frames. They are still subconsciously dealing with their former, and larger, dimensions. Many persons find themselves picking out clothes in their former, large sizes, even months after their excess weight has vanished.

UNSTRESSING YOUR LIFE

Although books on stress could fill a fair-sized library, it is still not completely understood. Stress is broadly defined as any change in the environment that requires some adjustment. Stress can be caused by noise, lack of sleep, achievement, nonachievement, losing a job, changing jobs, illness, surgery, child-birth, sexual activity—almost anything in life causes some stress. Many obese people react to stress by eating. Since continual eating will result in excess fat, it then follows that overweight people especially need a way to reduce the effect of stress or to avoid it. The program that follows is simple, workable, and in-volves a minimum of ritual activity.

1. Find a quiet place to relax. Lean back, close your eyes, and let your body totally relax. Imagine that your body has floated upward and is drifting along. Now you are gently settling down and coming to rest in the most natural and happy place for you. It may be on the beach with friends, in the mountains, or some other quiet and secluded spot, wherever you feel relaxed and happy. Remember the feeling and let it soak through your body.

2. From then on, when you get into a situation that makes you feel angry or nervous, stop right then. Take a few deep breaths, think about the relaxed and happy feeling you had, let the tensions drain out, then solve the problem.

3. To get a feeling of relaxation, lie back in a chair or on the floor. Starting with the muscles of your face, tighten each set and then relax them. Work your way down your arms, trunk, and the rest of the body. Often people have no idea what it feels like to be relaxed, so they must learn to feel the contrast between a tensed muscle and a relaxed one. After you have done the muscle-

tightening and relaxing drill for a week or so, you will begin to pick up the ability to go into deep relaxation simply by telling yourself to relax.

4. The final step is meditation, simply clearing the mind for a few minutes. Again, get started by finding a quiet place and letting all your muscles relax. Simply feel the breath going in and out your nose and repeat to yourself a key word, such as *relax*. Don't worry about blocking things out of your mind or thinking about anything in particular. Let the thoughts come and go, and don't make any particular effort to pursue them. At least two sessions of ten minutes a day are recommended, but any time that you can devote to such relaxation is a precious gift to yourself. Anyone who complains about not having this much time twice a day should take a good look at his schedule. If heads of corporations and of huge government bureaus can find the time, the odds are that you can.

STRESS REDUCTION BY ESCAPE

In addition to the techniques of stress reduction already discussed, there is another approach that sometimes escapes notice. If a situation is causing you to feel nervous and tense, perhaps there is some way the entire situation can be changed or avoided. The mother of one dieter was constantly belittling her, thereby making her angry and causing her to eat. The patient was married and lived away from the mother, but this did not keep constant and daily telephone abuse from being dumped on Claudia. A try at assertiveness by Claudia did not slow her mother down at all. She was so accustomed to abusing her daughter that she could not or would not stop. Claudia finally decided to avoid her mother for almost a year. She refused to visit her, and Claudia's husband would not let her visit their home. Telephone calls were refused. Finally it dawned on the mother that the message her daughter was sending her was "Get off my back or get out of my life!" The mother attempted to change her ways, and mother and daughter now get along quite well.

BEWARE OF FEEDERS

Feeders (See Appendix 8) are all around you every day, and you must learn to coexist with them. Be forewarned that some people will go to incredible lengths to sabotage a diet. They may act from unconscious motives or consciously or even maliciously, but expect even your best friends to argue, plead, cajole, and threaten you to get you to go off your diet "just this once."

Spouses and parents are among the worst feeders. A spouse particularly may feel threatened with the new slimness or his or her mate, and the dieting mate may become so anxious that the diet is endangered. A definite feeling of insecurity or jealousy is engendered in many when their spouses lose weight and become more attractive. The spouse may try to wreck the diet by harassment, by leaving food around, or by insisting that the other partner eat the wrong kinds of foods. One dieter's husband even threatened a divorce if she did not go back to her formerly fat self. She did not relent, and he divorced her eventually and married an even heavier woman than she had been.

Fortunately, life is rarely so dramatic as to force a decision between a spouse and a diet. More ordinary stress situations involve deadlines for an office worker that push him or her into weekend work and nibbling or a parent's constant juggling of car pools to meet the needs of three children who have to be in three parts of town at the same time.

We all tumble into the trap of "gottas"—I gotta do this, I gotta do that, and what will they think of me if I don't do this, and on and on, endlessly. In truth, relatively few imperatives exist in life. By reexamining why you do something, you often can find another way to arrive at the same goal, or you may find that an action is not necessary at all.

One of life's biggest unnecessary "gottas" is thinking you have got to eat just because a feeder pushes food in front of you. Defuse feeder activities, if possible, by trying to enlist the person's help. Point out that offering you food is not helping. Don't be defensive; just say, "No, thank you." And repeat this over and over. This parrot technique is powerful and effective.

If you find yourself unable to cope with a serious feeder, you might want to give him or her a copy of the letter in Appendix 8, which explains how you are hurt by his or her activities and how he or she can help you instead.

The amount of control each one of us has over our environment differs, but even a prisoner has some control over his life. The harrassed, car-pooling parent can perhaps find a bus that one child could take, or find some place closer to home that offers that same activity, or arrange to drive for two weeks straight and then have two weeks off. The amount of possible solutions to reduce stress are limitless, once you drop the idea that there is a fixed, immutable way that things must be done. First, realize that any change in your life will cause a certain amount of stress. Then realize that nothing is worth a stress that keeps you fat, angry, and unhappy. Be creative, change the situation, escape from it. Just as the Fabulous Fructose Diet can reshape your body, you can reshape your life.

One last thing, even a small reduction in stress or a small amount of assertiveness where none existed before is a victory. A series of small victories over stress and the beginnings of assertive behavior will eventually help you win the big war against fat and low self-esteem.

5

Staying on the Diet

Now THAT YOU have become thoroughly imbued with the spirit of the Fabulous Fructose Diet and have learned about the various systems of dieting—and presumably have chosen one system to follow—all that remains is to *stay on the diet*. You've been on this route before, you say? And you happen to know that this is the hardest part of dieting? Of course it is. Anyone can start a diet. Initial enthusiasm carries you through the first few days of dieting. But when the going gets rough, too often the diet goes. And too many diet books bid the reader farewell at this stage —just when the reader needs all the emotional support he or she can get. This chapter is devoted to giving you the support you need to to stay on FFD. It tells you how to stay on the diet. It contains everything from general suggestions to avoiding tempting places where food may be forced on you to handling some of the inevitable physical side effects that accompany any diet.

GET SOME HELP FROM A FRIEND

To avoid deviating from the diet, use a diet monitor, a friend or relative who can help assess your progress. This is in addition to your physician's monitoring. You need an objective person who can go over your diet diary with you and who can verify your success in losing weight. If you run into a problem, the diet monitor should *not* criticize you. His only function is to serve as a reality check. It is very human to start off with good intentions, then gradually slide into doing something else. A diet monitor can help you objectively review your behavior. Plan to meet with your diet monitor at least once a week for diary review.

If one of the purposes of meeting with a diet monitor is to review a diet diary, then there must be a diary to review. The diary does not have to be elaborate, just a simple notation of what you ate, when, where, and why. Get a small notepad and carry it with you everywhere. Write down what you eat *before* you eat it. This serves as one additional barrier against unplanned or impulse eating.

Go over the diary when you meet with your diet monitor to review your progress. Discuss your weaknesses and strengths regarding food—you will have noted them in the diary if you keep the suggested record. Work out ways to capitalize on your strengths and to avoid your weaknesses. If one strength, for example, is that you have really taken to your new exercise program, which you do religiously every morning, but a weakness is that you tend to have a small, forbidden snack every day right after work, then try to reschedule your exercise time to that dangerous period right after work. If you are sticking to the diet, but it isn't working, or you are not feeling as well as you should, perhaps you should make an additional appointment with your doctor to discuss adjusting some element of the diet. The most important thing to remember about the diary is to use it as an analytical tool to help you regulate yourself during the diet.

Finally, if your house is not yet fatproofed, do it now. The more difficult it is to eat the wrong foods, the better off you will be.

Reread Chapter 4 on eating behavior. Most overweight persons do not feel they have enough control over their lives, a fact that only compounds the problem of controlling weight. Some simple techniques for getting what you want from life are offered in Chapter 4. Practice these techniques. As the ability to express yourself improves, so will your efforts in controlling your weight.

TWO GUIDELINES FOR SUCCESSFUL DIETING

A well-known bariatrician who had been invited to attend a meeting on obesity sat by and watched as several persons offered their analyses of a case history involving a woman who was several hundred pounds overweight. Finally he was asked, "Why do you think she is fat?" He stood up, looked carefully around the room, and replied, "Because she eats too much."

His words contain all the truth you need to stay on a diet. In simplest terms, they boil down to the following two guidelines:

1. Eat everything specified on your diet. This is especially true of the protein requirements. Eating less will not speed up your progress, and it can cause you to become ill if done over a period of time. Protein levels are planned very precisely to keep the body from breaking down vital tissues such as muscle and internal organs. Eating less than prescribed will disrupt this balance.

2. If a food is not on the diet, do not put it into your mouth. Many items contain hidden sugars that cause fluid retention and at the same time halt the fat-burning process dead in its tracks. On the Fabulous Fructose Diet, you will be losing weight more rapidly and feeling better than you have in many years. Ask yourself if you want to jeopardize that for something you won't remember in a day. Trite as it may sound, make a copy of this motto and place it on your refrigerator and pantry doors: "A minute in the mouth, an hour in the stomach, and a lifetime on the hips."

SIDE EFFECTS OF THE DIET

Any major dieting effort causes some changes in your body chemistry. Some of these changes, such as bad breath, are physiological; others, such as insomnia, are psychological. Regardless of their cause, they are a small price to pay in any case for losing weight.

And keeping on excess weight in the long run will prove far more hazardous to your health than any of these side effects.

Most of the side effects described in the following pages will never happen to you; they never, in fact, happen to the majority of dieters. The side effects that do happen would also occur on any other diet. The detailed listing and explanations that follow are by way of preparing you, should any one occur. Should you have any of these side effects, they will be less upsetting to you if you know what causes them and how they are likely to take effect.

It is not necessary even to read this section right now. But you should be aware that help is offered—when you need it—for any of the following side effects.

Bad Breath

One of the exit pathways for ketones is the lungs. Many bariatricians monitor a dieter's ketone level by measuring the expired ketones in the breath with a ketone-sensing diet monitor. A doctor can, therefore, tell in some of the very low carbohydrate diets how closely someone is following the diet. Other ketones are eliminated through the urine. One way to avoid bad breath is to drink water. The more water you drink, the more ketones you will expel through the kidneys and the fewer through the lungs, in theory, at least. In addition to increased water intake, the use of carbohydrate-free mouthwashes may help. Breath sprays are suitable, too, but never use breath mints or chewing gum, as they contain sugar.

If your breath continues to bother you and is making you really uncomfortable, you can always switch to a diet with a larger fructose content and avoid the ketosis altogether. You will lose weight more slowly.

Energy Loss
This happens to some degree to dieters in every conceivable reducing diet, no matter how well-planned the diet is. Since energy loss is usually related to carbohydrate withdrawal, there is less chance of this happening on the FFD. The stress load is lower on the FFD, too, which also helps minimize this problem. Some energy loss may be psychological, a response to dieting and the adaptation required to do so. The deprival of part of one's food is a tremendous stress to many dieters, and this stress and its effects must be understood by the physician and the patient in terms of energy levels. Upward adjustment of the fructose intake is usually sufficient to defuse this problem before it becomes too great.

Headache and Nausea
Organic waste products generated as a result of massive amounts of fat being burned may cause headache and nausea. These symptoms are usually temporary and respond to time and increased fluid intake.

Insomnia
The tranquilizing effects of food and the effect of food withdrawal are never more clear than in the sleep disturbances that accompany some diets. Many

obese people have used food as a sleeping potion for years, and its withdrawal can cause insomnia. Using a portion of the day's food for a bedtime snack, along with some fructose, usually solves the problem.

Postural Hypotension

This is the medical name for a condition in which standing up abruptly from a flat or sitting position is accompanied by a marked, but brief, drop in the blood pressure. Persons with postural hypotension usually complain of dizziness when assuming an erect position. The dizziness is caused by a marked drop in salt from the body stores as a result of the diuretic effect of the diet. Your body will soon adapt, but be careful when you get up out of bed or out of a chair until you see how you are affected. Additional salt may be added at the discretion of your physician.

Dry Skin and Cold Intolerance

Both these conditions can be the result of a low-calorie diet. They could also result from other conditions that your doctor should have ruled out. If the problems still remain, a vitamin A supplement and a good moisturizing lotion should help the dry skin. Fructose usually will help the intolerance to cold, unless this condition is something you had to a lesser degree before beginning the diet. Intolerance to cold is highly individual and hard to quantitate so it is often hard to treat. If your intolerance developed with the diet, the best thing to do is to grit your teeth and dress warmly. Increased exercise also helps.

Abdominal Gas and Constipation

These problems are side effects of any low-calorie or low-residue diet. Antacids with simethicone are sometimes effective for the abdominal gas. Over-the-counter digestive enzymes can help with poor digestion, but they are not cure-alls. One of the sugarless stool-softener products recommended by a druggist may be in order for constipation. (Observe all precautions on the labels.)

High water intake, walking or other exercise, elimination of as much stress as possible, and a high bulk intake all help the digestion and bowel patterns as much as anything. Avoid all powdered laxatives and bulking agents for they contain entirely too much carbohydrate for someone on the FFD or on the maintenance program.

Menstrual Irregularities

Regular menstrual cycles depend on a very delicate balance of hormones, and any stress, including a reducing diet, can upset this balance. In very obese women, the menses may have ceased, and the diet may cause them to begin again. In less overweight women, there may be some irregularity. The menstrual flow may be heavier, lighter, or stop altogether. In the vast majority of cases, there are no changes at all. It is only the unknown that startles people. In all cases, the cycle should return to your normal pattern when you finish the diet.

Remember that if there is even the slightest chance that you are pregnant, you should not be on this or any weight-reduction diet. Have a pregnancy test if you suspect that you are pregnant. Use some type of birth-control precaution while on the diet if you are sexually active or anticipate that you may be.

Hair-Growth Problems

Hair goes through a three-phase cycle: it grows, goes into a resting phase, then finally disconnects from the blood supply and falls out. The cycle repeats itself. In low-calorie diets, the resting phase is sometimes speeded up, and more hair appears to be lost than usual. This tendency can be partially overcome by keeping the protein intake high, another reason to eat all the protein ordered for you. This hair loss is not permanent, and it merely represents an acceleration of a natural process. It does not happen to everyone, but it does occur occasionally. Going on and off a diet repeatedly and not sticking to it properly encourages this effect. The normal growth cycle will resume when you complete the diet, and many people find their hair is healthier than before the diet.

Diarrhea or Loose Stools

One desirable effect of fructose is its slow absorption from the intestine back into the bloodstream. An occasional problem arises from the retained water and the fructose inside the intestinal tract. This can lead to what is called osmotic diarrhea. Since the extra fluid stimulates the intestine to be more active and so move the fructose and bowel contents through it quicker there is a greater chance of getting diarrhea. The symptom is short-lived and usually vanishes after a few days. If diarrhea occurs, cut the fructose down and gradually increase in small amounts until the original intake amount is reached. For temporary relief of diarrhea, consult your doctor or a pharmacist for a sugar-free medication that can be dispensed without prescription. Be sure to follow the directions and precautions on the label.

Coping with a Cold or Flu

A cold or bout of flu is no reason to drop the Fabulous Fructose Diet. The diet supplies any nutrients you need to get well just as quickly as you would on a regular diet. A cold will usually clear up in about seven days no matter what you do with it. You do need to be careful about any medication you take. Many cold and flu medicines, particularly the liquids, contain sugar or caffeine. The only sugar-free cough syrups are available by prescription only. Syrupy medications are usually a real tip off to high-sugar content. Many of the so-called sugar-free cough syrups contain sorbitol, a definite no at this time. Read the labels, too, on throat medicines. Do not use any type of lozenges or throat-numbing candy drops as they all contain too much sugar. Gargling with a warm salt-water solution is effective and cheap. You may also use any form of aspirin or acetaminophen for the relief of fever or aching. Avoid those tablets with caffeine, and follow the precautions on the package or bottle.

Fruit juice, whiskey, honey, vinegar, and any combination of these are not the type of cold remedies that are going to help you while on the diet. If you desire it, you can get all the vitamin C you need from tablets and capsules. These vitamin C products can be obtained from most health food stores and pharmacies. Fruit juices have no place on the diet until the maintenance stage.

If your illness persists, see your doctor. Explain that you are on a low-carbohydrate diet and would prefer sugar-free preparations. The best prescription for colds is rest, which does not include stocking up on high-calorie food. Chicken soup, broth, or your favorite dessert are not going to make you well any sooner. Sugarless herb teas may be a good fluid source during this time. Appendix 9 contains more information and the names of suggested cold medication to use.

Possibly too much attention has been paid to the side effects of the FFD or any strenuous diet. Most dieters sail through diets with none of these problems. Still, knowing in advance what might happen is like insurance: it puts you in the right state of mind to cope with it and lessens the chances that any side effect will discourage you enough to put you off the diet. And when measured against the wear and tear on your body that comes from carrying around excess baggage year after year, these side effects are all minimal.

6

Staying Thin Forever

THROUGH AN ENORMOUS amount of effort, you have now taken off the weight that plagued you for so long. Now you must learn to keep it off—forever.

Keeping off weight has been a major problem in weight control, probably because so few dieters change their life-styles and eating patterns to insure that their weight loss will be permanent.

Your chances of successful, permanent weight loss are better if you have a realistic picture of what must be done to control your weight. Overweight is a problem that can be controlled. It is not, however, something you will outgrow, something that, once conquered, will never again return. Obesity is a persistent problem because it is so closely tied to your life-style, your attitudes about food and exercise, and even your attitude about life in general.

Being thin forever means that you will have to be on guard for the rest of your life not to return to your old eating habits, which are guaranteed to put on your lost weight. Being thin forever involves a three-step program: (1) a new, permanent pattern of eating, (2) a revision of old eating and living habits, and (3) the addition of new, health-insuring habits that will help control your bad eating patterns.

The new eating pattern involves learning to substitute fructose for other kinds of sweets in your diet. It involves always eating fewer carbohydrates than you did in your fat days and learning to fill up on vegetables, salads, and protein foods.

The revision of old habits comes from a recognition of your perception of food and the sensation of hunger. Even taking into account the physiological problems associated with the hunger that result when you are caught in the glucose-insulin trap, most fat persons rarely experience true hunger or even, for that matter, true relief from hunger, or satiety. Much of what you perceive as hunger is simply a habitual response to external food cues—the time of day, the amount of time since your last meal ("It's been three hours since breakfast—I must be hungry"), the sight or smell of food.

The Transition Diet offers an excellent opportunity to retrain yourself and test your strength regarding any new habits you will need to keep off extra, unwanted weight. Learn to listen to your body, to distinguish between real and imagined hunger. Real hunger will not get you into trouble, because a small meal will satisfy it. Imagined hunger, or psychologically induced hunger, has no true physical basis, so you can eat a lot when dealing with this kind of hunger without feeling satisfied. This psychological hunger is what causes problems in keeping weight off forever.

Learn what weakens or threatens you enough to make you want to eat, and then develop some new life patterns for avoiding those stresses. If the stresses cannot be avoided, look for substitutes other than food to ease the pain. When your formerly fat self would have run out to buy and gorge herself or himself on a candy bar, your new, slender self will plan to use a fructose serving in a beverage, or better yet, to work out a reward that has nothing at all to do with food.

Help in retraining eating habits comes from a book titled *Habits, Not Diet* by James M. Ferguson, M.D. (Bull Publishing Company, Palo Alto, Calif.). Written in a programmed-instruction format, the book contains a diary that covers twenty weeks, during which time a dieter can examine his eating patterns.

Breaking through the fat barriers to become a new, slender person can be a frightening experience. While this should be your most glorious moment, it is actually a time of great weakness for most dieters. Psycologists have noted that many persons have a need to fail. They cannot adjust to the reality of success, and they panic when they are close to a special goal. For years, you may have been telling yourself, "If only I lost twenty pounds, then I would be able to . . ." Whatever it is that you have wanted to do, don't get this close and lose your way. Remember how hard you have worked to get this far, and use your new powers of self-control to insure your continued success.

Breaking through the glucose-insulin trap and eluding the false hunger that makes so many fat persons compulsive gluttons has been enough to launch many persons into entirely new lives. "Imagery is great, but I've finally got the real thing," one mother of two reported in an exultant tone. "After years of trying to lose, I'm finally the person I want to be." Armed with her new self-confidence and the knowledge that she had succeeded in one of the toughest of all possible human endeavors, she went on to change other facets of her life. Today, she has a new career, writing articles for a local newspaper. She plays a tough game of tennis, and she still has time and energy left over for her family and friends, a marked change from her old, fat-laden days when all her energy was required simply to make it through another day.

The rewards are too great if you have made it this far to give up now. And one helpful aspect of the FFD is that it sees you through the transition stage via the Fructose Transition Diet to a new permanent eating style and a lifetime maintenance plan.

WHY THE TRANSITION DIET IS NEEDED

Gradual transition and planned eating is particularly important when weaning yourself off any of the Fabulous Fructose Diets. Putting carbohydrates other than fructose back into the diet too quickly will act as a dam and retain an increased amount of body water, producing weight gain. The faster the carbohydrates are added back, the faster weight will increase. Because of this, the transition program should not begin until you are 5 pounds under your target weight. You can expect temporary 5- to 10-pound weight gain when the extra carbohydrates are added; this is something you need to be prepared for mentally and physically, and being under your target weight helps. The transition diet is still a reducing diet and will remove a few more pounds while the physiological water gain is adding some weight to the body.

Introducing sugars and starches gradually is also important because a carbohydrate binge could temporarily overrun the fluid-balance mechanism, producing a weight gain of 15 pounds or more in extreme cases. For example, a pancake breakfast, followed by lunch with baked potato and ice cream could cause a weight gain of 6 to 10 pounds overnight because of fluid being held in the tissues. This can devastate you and possibly cause you to feel you have lost weeks of effort. Some dieters are pushed into an orgy of unplanned eating if they are not prepared for the gain. There have also been some reports of gallbladder colic attacks following the too-abrupt reintroduction of carbohydrates and fatty foods into the diet.

HOW THE TRANSITION DIET WORKS

The Transition Diet carries you through the transition stage between one of the full-scale FFD systems to the permanent eating plan that will keep you slim for life. The length of time you will stay on the Transition Diet depends upon the FFD system you have been using to lose weight. If you have been on the Basic Fructose Diet or the Fructose Vegetarian Diet, begin with week one of the Transition Diet and proceed through week six. If you have followed the Meals-and-Munch Diet, begin at week three. If you have been on the Dependable Diet, begin at week four.

The Transition Diet contains the same basic components as do the other diet systems. The amount and variety of List 4 vegetables are increased, and some starchy vegetables can be eaten.

A final word of advice before you start the Transition Diet: follow the diet as exactly as possible. It has an extensive history of successful use and is exactly what you need to start your new slim lifestyle. Plunging back into the old ways of eating only insures that your formerly fat, lifeless body will return to torture you.

First, the basic diet plan is described, followed by the lists of protein, vegetable, milk, and fruit food shares.

The Diet Plan

Week One

Add one serving of a List 4 vegetable and one additional protein share to each day's food intake. Fructose and salads remain the same. Keep drinking plenty of water and taking the same amount of vitamins, potassium, and other minerals as in the diet you were on.

Week Two

Add one more serving of a List 4 vegetable and one serving per day of a vegetable from List 5. Add one more protein share. Supplemental vitamins, potassium, and other minerals remain the same. Fructose is unchanged.

Week Three

Add one serving of fruit. At this point, you can cut the potassium in half. (If on 10 milliequivalents, go to 5, etc.) Everything else remains the same.

Week Four

Add another serving of List 5 vegetables. At this point, you can cut out all supplemental potassium. Continue taking other vitamins and minerals.

Week Five

Add one grain share to the day's intake, perhaps as a snack at night or with breakfast.

Week Six

You will now be eating two extra shares of List 4 vegetables, two shares of List 5 vegetables, one fruit, and one grain serving. You are on two extra shares of protein daily and on the previously ordered vitamins and minerals. Reduce the intake of fructose to 30 grams per day. The RDA vitamins and minerals should be continued for the rest of your life.

A special note concerning the Meals-and-Munch Diet: begin at week three, as already noted, and eat six days a week as you have been eating on Tuesday, Thursday, and Saturday. Sunday stays the same during the entire six weeks of transition.

FRUCTOSE

The full amount of fructose is taken until week six, when the full amounts of the fruit and protein supplements have been added to the diet. At this time, 30 to 60 grams are usually still recommended, although the actual amount varies with the number of carbohydrates you eat. The section on fructose under the permanent diet shows how to calculate exact fructose needs at this point.

Food Shares for the Transition Diet

The following lists are comparable to those used in the other FFD systems, although, of course, they are not interchangeable. Remember to stay within the specified quantities on the list and to prepare the foods as noted, that is, either cooked or uncooked.

VEGETABLES

LIST 4 VEGETABLES

One share equals one 8-ounce, loosely packed measuring cup of *uncooked food*. It may be eaten as a salad or snack during the day. Dressings, if used, are the same as those permitted on the Basic Fructose Diet.

Bean sprouts
Cabbage
Cauliflower
Celery
Chicory
Cucumbers
Dandelion or
   beet greens
Dill pickles
Escarole

Lettuce (any type)
Mushrooms
Peppers, red
   and green
Radishes
Sauerkraut (with no
   sugar added)
Spinach
Tomatoes

LIST 5 VEGETABLES

One share equals one-half of an 8-ounce, loosely packed measuring cup of cooked food.

Asparagus
Broccoli
Brussels sprouts
Cabbage
Cauliflower
Chard
Collard greens
Dandelion or
   beet greens
Eggplant

Kale
Mushrooms
Mustard greens
Okra
Rhubarb
Spinach
String beans
Summer squash
Tomatoes
Turnip greens

FRUIT LIST

All fruits should be fresh; no dried, canned, or frozen fruits are permitted.

Apple 1 medium
(3-inch diameter)
Apricots 2
Banana ½ small
Blackberries,
blueberries, or
raspberries ½ cup
Cantaloupe ¼
Cherries 8 large

Grapefruit ½
Honeydew ¼
medium
Orange 1
Peach 1 medium
Pear 1 small
Strawberries
¾ cup
Watermelon 1 cup

No fruit juices are allowed on the Transition Diet.

BREADLIKE OR GRAINLIKE LIST

Baked potato, 1 small, no butter or other topping
and no sour cream, bacon bits, or chives
Bread, whole wheat 1 slice
Cooked cereal: oatmeal, cream of wheat, farina
½ cup, no milk permitted
Corn, cornmeal, or grits, 2 rounded tablespoons
Green peas, ½ cup
Muffin, whole wheat 1 small (2-inch diameter)
Zucchini, ½ cup

MILK PRODUCTS LIST

Unflavored yogurt, no sugar added by manufac-
turer, 1 cup (You may add fructose or fruit, if
desired. See recipes in Appendix 5.)
Cottage cheese 1 cup
Farmer or hoop cheese 1 ounce

PROTEIN

Use the lists of protein shares on the Basic Fructose Diet or the meatlike foods on the Vegetarian Fructose Diet, if you are following that.

DESSERTS

For dessert you may have one-half cup of D-Zerta Gelatin (not pudding) each day, beginning with week three. One portion of Cooper's cheesecake or Cooper's cannoli, every two to four days, depending on your level of activity, may be started during week four. Remember to count the fructose used in making these desserts and subtract this amount from the total grams you are permitted.

Meals and Snacks During Transition

On the Transition Diet, plan on three main meals with three small snacks during times when hunger is a problem. Meals and snacks should come from the allowed lists of foods.

Seasonings

The use of salt in the diet should be cautious. While on the low-carbohydrate intake, there is a natural diuretic action that takes place in the body, but once full carbohydrate consumption is resumed, salt intake should stay low until the body has adapted to the change. Ignoring this instruction can result in unneeded fluid retention, bloating, and discomfort.

The use of salt substitutes or Lite Salt in judicious quantities is a good alternative. You will derive a certain amount of salt satiety and have less water retention. Lite Salt has sodium but in lesser amounts than does regular table salt. If twice as much Lite Salt as usual is put on foods, however, there is the same amount of fluid retention and bloating.

LIFETIME MAINTENANCE

The Permanent Diet is meant to be a lifetime proposition. If that sounds depressing, you should remember two things. First, no one is perfect, and there will be times when you will go off the diet for one reason or another. This is no reason to backslide permanently, though, and a night or a week off the diet is no excuse for not returning to it immediately. Second, no single diet can take into account the individual preferences of all persons, so you may have to adjust the diet somewhat to meet your personal needs. Feel free to do so as long as you are able to maintain your target weight.

The Permanent Diet offers a great deal of variety and more food than you can probably eat. Although it is called a diet, it is mostly a maintenance plan to get you through the rest of your life as the slender person you truly want to be.

Losing weight—either 10 pounds or 100 pounds— is a tremendous accomplishment. To do so, you have learned to change your eating and your living patterns. At moments of weakness—when you have gained 5 pounds, and going on one of the diet systems seems like too much effort—think back to how much effort you put into losing the weight. With careful eating habits, you will never again have to go through the process of dieting for more than a few days at a time. Think about how much you enjoy the new, slender person you have become. Think about the pleasure of being able to control your eating habits. And when you are done thinking, go for a long walk until the urge to eat something you should not eat has vanished.

If you could successfully accomplish so major a task as taking off weight, then you certainly are strong enough to keep the weight off—forever.

Maintaining a Record of Weight

A record of your weight is important because it will protect you from creeping obesity, a common problem following successful weight loss. Everyone's weight fluctuates from day to day and sometimes from hour to hour, and, unfortunately, the scale is not a very accurate way to estimate the amount of fat in the human body. For consistency, during the first two weeks of the maintenance diet try to weigh yourself every morning after emptying your bladder and before you dress. After that, begin to weigh less frequently, until by the end of the second month, you are only weighing once a week.

Write these weights down, perhaps in a notebook kept in the bathroom for this purpose. If you go more than one pound over your base or target figure, start writing down everything you eat or drink that has calories.

Also, when your weight creeps up go back to daily

weigh-ins until the weight has stayed at your target level or lower for a week, then resume your old schedule. If your weight has climbed too rapidly, go back to one of the FFD systems until your target weight is reached again.

Protein in the Permanent Diet

A large variety of different types of protein foods are available, and everyone can find an adequate amount of good protein to satisfy his or her individual taste. Many of the items on the meatlike list are not meat and are not even usually thought of as meat-type foods. Getting a variety of protein foods, however, insures that all the essential amino acids, or building blocks for body protein, are available each day. On a vegetarian diet, getting the right combination of food to satisfy the body's protein needs can be tricky, which explains the many protein foods on this eating plan.

Several items in the meatlike shares should only be used sparingly, usually once a week at most. These include the cold cuts and peanut butter.

Measuring Your Food

Try to use standard serving measurements or their metric equivalents for accuracy. They include a tea-spoon (5 ml.), a tablespoon (15 ml.), a fluid ounce (30 ml.), a measuring cup (240 ml.) or its fractions (¼ cup or 2 ounces or 60 ml. and ½ cup or 4 ounces or 120 ml.).

A good idea is to use the measuring cup to measure out some dry material such as rice or peas. After you have measured enough food, your eye will become good enough to make judgments about the size of portions. Remember, accuracy and self-honesty are the best weapons against creeping obesity.

A similar method can be used to measure food slices. Cut out pieces of cardboard or paper that correspond to the sizes of meat or bread portions and keep them for reference until your eye can measure accurately.

If your portions are all size controlled, and if eating is only done at meal time with you in command, you should have no trouble in keeping your weight at the desired level. Your food should be selected so that the total diet is high in protein, low in fat, and moderate in carbohydrates. The only simple sugar you should eat is fructose.

Getting Exercise

Activity is still very important. A brisk twenty-minute walk results in about an extra 100-calorie deficit each day or about an extra pound lost per month. If you have been gaining a steady 3 pounds a year on your present diet and change nothing else but your walking habit, you can end up after a year with about 9 pounds less fat. Another possibility, when you reach your desired weight, is to add the twenty-minute walks daily to "earn" an extra treat.

Little efforts are also important. Parking a few blocks from work, or at the farthest point in a parking lot at a shopping center, are also good ways to increase one's daily caloric expenditure. Walking up and down

stairs in a building is also healthy. Add to this your
daily walk or run and perhaps an exercise or dance
class, and you have a good start in reprogramming
your activity pattern so that you will stay thin forever.

Fructose, Sugar, and You

One food that you would be wise to omit from your
table forever is sugar—plain, regular table sugar.
Even the so-called natural, or raw, sugars are still
sugar and can start you on the path to the glucose-
insulin trap again.

Just because something is sold in the health foods
section of a grocery store or in a health food store
does not mean it is healthy for you. A lot of the
granola cereals and other granola products have loads
of sugar in them. Other natural products also may
contain sugar, so if you are going to avoid sugar,
learn to be a careful label reader.

Another helpful path to healthy eating is to try to
eat grains only in their natural state. Avoid enriched
or bleached, overprocessed flours. When possible, buy
or make breads using whole wheat or whole grain
flour. Again, learn to read labels carefully; some
manufacturers make a whole wheat bread that consists primarily of white flour with a tiny amount of
whole grain flour and a lot of artificial caramel color-
ing added to produce a brown-colored bread that costs
a lot and has no advantage over regular white bread.

Try to avoid such high-sugar foods as pancakes,
pastries, pies, and cakes. The best dessert for food

addicts is fruit, either in its natural state or sprinkled with some fructose granules.

If you feel the need to eat sweets—and you will occasionally—use fructose or saccharin. As long as you remain within the limit in grams of fructose permitted each day, there is no reason not to use it as a condiment. Fructose can also be stretched with the use of saccharin. In a cup of coffee, for example, nine grams of fructose alone or six grams of fructose with ¼ grain of saccharin produces the same sweetness as sugar does.

When using fructose as a sweetener or sugar substitute, remember that it does contain four calories per gram. Use too much and you have defeated the purpose of the diet.

While on the Maintenance Diet—the rest of your life!—take fructose in small doses, usually 5 or 6 grams, throughout the day. Thirty minutes before meals and about two hours after meals are the best times for taking fructose in order to suppress your appetite successfully and maintain your energy level on an even keel. A popular way to take it is in a glass of sugar-free lemonade or Kool-Aid.

Remember the list of forbidden sweeteners and avoid them as much as possible. These include sorbitol, mannitol, xylitol, glucose, lactose, and dextrose. When a food label contains one of these ingredients, avoid it.

As has been pointed out, the simple sugars have only two fates in the body: they are stored as fat, or they are used for energy. This means that if you take in too much of any sugar—even fructose—your body

will convert it to fat. An increase in fat, or triglycerides, circulating in the blood stream, is known
to be a risk factor in heart disease and related problems. At a level of 100 grams or less of fructose a
day, the likelihood of your having problems with increased triglycerides is almost nonexistent. Still,
checking with your family doctor for triglycerides and
cholesterol tests prior to going on the FFD is a good
idea, particularly if you are over thirty and have a
family or personal history of heart or blood-vessel
disease.

The Diet Plan

Before going over this Permanent Diet, calculate
your approximate calorie needs per day. Unless you
are unusually active or inactive, a good way to figure
your calorie needs is to use the information in Appendix 3. After finding the number of calories that
you should burn each day, study Table 6–1 to see how
many shares in each category you can have to equal
your daily needs for energy. At this level, if figured
correctly, you should maintain your weight within
rather strict limits from week to week. If you either
gain or lose significantly over a period of a week, you
may need to adjust the calories up or down until you
find the right level to maintain your ideal weight.

Do not attempt to swap items in one group for
those in another. This is a sure way to failure. The
amounts listed in the share groups are equal to one
share. Each share in a group has approximately the
same calories, protein, fat, and carbohydrates.

LIST 1 VEGETABLES

These vegetables are the same as in the Transition Diet (List 4). They have negligible calories and carbohydrates if raw. If cooked, they become List 2 Vegetables. In the Permanent Diet, they are permitted in unlimited amounts when consumed raw.

LIST 2 VEGETABLES

These vegetables are also the same as in the Transition Diet (List 5). All are served cooked. Their caloric content and their available carbohydrates are greater when cooked, so they must be measured. One share is equal to one-half cup, loosely packed.

LIST 3 VEGETABLES

This last group of vegetables has the highest caloric and carbohydrate content of all, except for the bread-like vegetables that are listed with breads and similar foods. One serving is still a loosely packed, one-half cup. The quantities are the same, whether cooked or raw. You should have only one serving a day or less from this list. Never exceed this limit.

Beets	Onions	Turnips
Carrots	Pumpkin	Winter squash
Green peas	Rutabagas	Zucchini

NOTE: On the Permanent Diet, vegetables may be fresh, frozen, or canned as long as sugar or syrup has not been used in the preparation.

FRUIT LIST

Each portion below contains the same amount of calories and carbohydrates. Quantities are given in household measurements. One cup equals 8 fluid ounces.

Apple	1 small (2-inch diameter)
Apple juice, unsweetened	⅜ cup
Apple sauce, homemade only	½ cup
Apricots, fresh	2 medium
Apricots, dried	4 halves
Banana	½ small
Berries, fresh, frozen, or water-packed (strawberry, raspberry, or blackberry)	1 cup
Blueberries	⅔ cup
Cantaloupe (6-inch diameter)	¼ melon
Cherries	10 large
Dates, no sugar glaze or coating	2 dates
Figs, fresh	2 large
Figs, dried, no glaze or coating	1 small
Grapefruit	½ small

Grapefruit juice, unsweetened only	½ cup
Grapes, any variety	12
Grape juice, unsweetened only	¼ cup
Honeydew melon (7-inch diameter)	⅛ melon
Mango	½ small
Orange	1 small
Orange juice, unsweetened only	½ cup
Papaya	⅓ medium
Peach	1 medium
Pear	1 small
Pineapple, fresh or water-packed	½ cup
Pineapple juice, unsweetened only	⅓ cup
Plums	2 medium
Prunes, no glaze or sweetener	2 medium
Raisins, no glaze or sweetener	2 level tablespoons
Tangerine	1 large
Watermelon	1 cup

NOTE: Apple sauce, bananas, dates, grape juice, and raisins are only permitted once a week and only one share of each is allowed for that week. A part of the daily fructose ration may be used to add sweetness to any of the above.

BREADLIKE OR GRAINLIKE LIST

Each of these items, though they may not be what you think of as bread, have a composition similar to bread. Each food is almost completely composed of carbohydrate, along with a small amount of protein per share. Cooked or uncooked, the nutritional value is roughly the same.

Bagel, preferably whole wheat or rye	½
Baked beans, no pork	¼ cup
Beans, dry, cooked (kidney, lima, navy, pigeon, pinto, butter, black)	½ cup
Biscuit or roll	1 (2-inch diamter)
Bread, whole wheat or rye	1 slice
Breadfruit or tanniers	1 small
Cereal, cooked, no sugar added	½ cup
Cereal, dry, no sugar or glaze added (flakes or puffed form)	¾ cup
Corn	⅓ cup
Cornbread, no sugar added	1½-inch cube

Corn on the cob	½ ear
Cornstarch (for use in cooking)	2 level tablespoons or less, as recipe notes
Crackers, round (Ritz type)	6 to 8 (1½-inch diameter)
Flour, preferably whole wheat or cornmeal	2½ level tablespoons
Graham crackers	2 (2-inch square)
Muffin	1 (2-inch diameter)
Oyster crackers	20 (½ cup)
Parsnips	⅔ cup
Peas, dry, cooked (split, cowpeas, black-eyed, chick)	½ cup
Plantain, green	¼
Potato, sweet or yam, baked or boiled (no candied or sugar glaze)	¼ cup
Potato, white, baked or boiled only	1 small (2-inch diameter)
Rice, hominy grits, or noodles (cooked)	½ cup
Saltine crackers	5 (2-inch square)
Soda crackers	3 (2½-inch square)
Soybeans, cooked or dry roasted	¼ cup
Spaghetti, macaroni, and other pasta (cooked)	½ cup

| Tortilla | 1 regular, flour or cornmeal |

FAT LIST

Like the bread list, the fat list contains things you may not think of as fat, but your body treats them as if they were. The fat and caloric content is identical for each of these.

Achiote spice, prepared (Spanish spice)	1 level teaspoon
Avocado	⅛ small
Bacon, crisp and drained	1 slice
Butter or margarine	1 teaspoon or 1 pat
Cream, heavy	1 tablespoon
Cream, light	2 tablespoons (1 ounce)
Cream cheese	1 level tablespoon
Mayonnaise or mayonnaise-like salad dressing	1 level teaspoon
Oil (safflower, sesame, soybean, peanut, olive, corn) or cooking fat (lard and shortening)	1 level teaspoon
Olives	5 small

NOTE: Regular bottled salad dressing and nuts have been eliminated from the Permanent Diet for at least the first two years, because of their possible addictive qualities. Six small nuts make up a single fat share, an impossibly small amount of nuts to consume and then stop. Diet dressings averaging six or less calories per tablespoon are permitted.

MILK LIST

The milk list consists of fermented and unfermented milk products. Where possible, try not to consume any more whole milk, whether low-fat or not, than absolutely necessary. The lactose content is considerable, and the glucose and galactose each eventually contribute somewhat to the glucose-insulin trap.

You will notice that cheese and cottage cheese appear on this list as well as on the meatlike share list. Because of the unique position of these fermented products, they can be used on either. For instance, on a 1,500 calorie diet you have two milk shares and three-and-a-half meat shares a day. You could use 3 ounces of cheddar cheese to provide part of your meat shares and one cup of yogurt along with 6 tablespoons of cottage cheese to provide the two milk shares. When you see the symbol (F) after a milk share, it indicates a lesser fat content and means you can add two extra fat shares for each (F) share used.

Blue cheese, Camembert, cheddar, fontina, Gorgonzola, gouda, Gruyère, Monterey Jack, Parmesan, Roquefort, Stilton, Swiss cheese	1 ounce
Buttermilk, made with low-fat milk (F)	1 cup
Cottage cheese, creamed	6 tablespoons
Cottage cheese, (F) uncreamed	6 tablespoons
Evaporated milk	½ cup
Low-fat cheese (Edam, mozzarella, ricotta, Liederkranz) (F)	1 ounce
Nonfat dry milk, reconstituted (F)	1 cup
Skim, low-fat, or 2 percent milk (F)	1 cup
Whole milk	1 cup
Yogurt, made with low-fat milk (F)	1 cup (If flavoring is desired, use recipes in Appendix 5.)

Here is an example of the use of the (F) symbol:
a person who is permitted two milk shares a day and
chooses 2 ounces of Edam cheese for these requirements is entitled to four extra fat shares—for example, two pieces of bacon and two extra pats of
butter.

MEAT LIST
Some of the items on this list are obviously not
meat, but the protein and fat content are approximately the same as meat, so they are grouped with
meat for convenience. Those items marked with a
(W) are permitted only in the amount of one share
per week because of their high carbohydrate content.
More than that amount is not a good idea and gives
more of the wrong kind of carbohydrates than desirable. The meatlike foods are grouped into three
lists. List 1 meats have a lower fat content and fewer
calories per share. List 2 meats have more saturated
fats and more calories but still offer a good quality
protein. List 3 meats, while being higher in calories
and saturated fats and containing some carbohydrates, are still acceptable as protein food and can
make up a smaller part of weekly diet.

LIST 1 MEATS

Almost all the items and the quantities necessary
to make up one protein share are listed in Chapter 3,
table 3–2. These include clams, cod, crabmeat, haddock, halibut, flounder, lobster, water-packed tuna,
and salmon. Additional foods include:

Cottage cheese, any style	½ cup
Eggs, boiled, poached, scrambled, or fried without fat	2 large
Low-fat cheese (Edam, mozzarella, ricotta, Liederkranz)	2 ounces

LIST 2 MEATS

Again, almost all the items and the quantity needed to make one protein share are listed in table 3–2. Protein sources include beef, veal, poultry, liver, lamb, shrimp, and scallops. Additional foods include:

Cheese with higher fat content (blue cheese, Camembert, cheddar, fontina, Gorgonzola, Gouda, Gruyère, Monterey Jack, Parmesan, Swiss cheese, Roquefort, Stilton)	2 ounces

LIST 3 MEATS

These are less desirable, but still usable, protein items. The amount necessary to make one serving of the pork and ham items is also in Table 3–2. The rest follow. Each quantity represents one protein share, except for peanut butter, which can only be eaten in a smaller portion.

Cold cuts (W)	2 slices (4½-inches square by ⅛-inch thick)
Frankfurter (W)	2
Peanut butter, any style (W)	2 tablespoons equals ½ share
Sardines	6 medium, well-drained

THE ALL-YOU-WANT-WITHIN-REASON LIST

Seasonings: celery salt, garlic, garlic salt, lemon juice, mustard, mint, nutmeg, parsley, pepper, and all other noncaloric herbs and spices; saccharin in tablet or liquid form, vanilla, vinegar, and sugar-free bouillon.

Other Foods: Fat-free broth, unflavored gelatin, rennet tablets, sour or dill pickles, cranberries without sugar, decaffeinated coffee, herb teas.

THE NO-MORE-THAN-ONE-TEASPOONFUL-A-DAY LIST

Certain foods such as catsup, soy sauce, cocktail sauce, steak sauce, horseradish, barbecue sauce, and tartar sauce are permitted, provided that no more than one teaspoonful per day of any one of these is used. Explore the world of calorie-free spices and lemon juice as an alternative to these high-carbohydate condiments.

MAINTENANCE FOR VEGETARIANS

The diet described in *Diet for a Small Planet*, by Frances Moore Lappé, is an excellent source for vegetarians. By using the vegetarian meatlike foods listed in *Diet for a Small Planet* and in this book, the protein needs of the body can be met. Additional vegetables, fruits, fats, milk products, and grainlike foods can be added to the diet by using the lists in this chapter.

Prepared Foods

You probably have noticed that fast-food restaurant products are not included in any of these share lists: neither are canned soups, stews, and chili. You will at times be tempted or forced to eat such foods. For that reason, caloric values for some of these foods are listed in Barbara Kraus's books. They are not recommended until you have been on the Permanent Diet for at least six months to a year.

Meat shares on the Permanent Diet are fewer than

on the reducing-diet systems because of the use of other foods that contain protein, such as milk and breadlike foods. Table 6–1 gives the daily number of shares and the amount of fructose permitted for daily caloric intakes of from 800 to 2,600 calories. (If your needs are greater than 2,600 calories, check with your physician or ADA dietician for additional share allocations to make up for the deficit.)

Fructose can be eaten in any of the forms previously permitted, or in candies or pastries listed in Appendix 5. Whenever fructose is used as a topping on fruit or in a sweet recipe, it must be counted as part of the daily allotment.

TABLE 6-1.
Daily Caloric Needs

Calories	Vegetables List 2	Vegetables List 3	Fruit	Bread	Meat	Fat	Milk	Fructose Grams/Day
800	1	0	1	1	2½	0	1½	10
900	1	1	1	1½	2½	0	1½	14
1000	1	1	1½	1½	2½	0	1½	34
1100	1	1	2	1½	2½	0	2	34
1200	2	1	2	2	2½	0	2	40
1300	2	1	2	2½	3	0	2	40
1400	2	1	2	3	3	1	2	43
1500	2	1	2	3	3½	2	2	43
1600	2	1	2	3½	4	2	2	43
1700	2	1	2	3½	4½	2	2	43
1800	2	1	2	4½	4½	3	2	43
1900	2	1	2	4½	5	3	2	45
2000	2	1	2	5	5½	3	2	45
2100	3	1	2	5	5½	4	2	50
2200	3	1	2	6	5½	5	2	50
2300	3	1	3	7	5½	5	2	50
2400	3	1	3	8	5½	5	2	50
2500	3	1	3½	8	5½	5	2½	50
2600	3	1	4	8	6	5	2½	50

7

All Your Questions Answered

ASSUME THAT the world's greatest expert on weight control is sitting beside you on an airplane. You have a chance to ask him anything you want. If personal experience and opinion surveys regarding weight control are any guide, most of your questions would be based on misapprehensions and downright nonsense. Getting usable information depends more on asking the right questions than on having an expert on hand.

Why a person eats too much and how this knowledge can be useful to a dieter is the subject of this chapter. Constructive thought about weight control starts with the understanding that excess weight results from more food fuel going into the body than is expended through the needs of basal metabolism or physical activity. That fact established, we can now look at how and why people eat too much or why they fail to recognize a stopping point.

The first question most persons ask about weight is an easy one.

Question: "I eat like a bird, yet I can't stop gaining," or, "I never eat anything, yet I'm still fat. Do you think my weight could be caused by a glandular problem?"

Answer: Physicians are fond of pointing out that birds eat their own weight in food every day. If the human metabolism produced a body temperature of 110 degrees or if people spent their days flying under their own power, they could afford to eat like birds. Less than one percent of all obesity problems that doctors see are caused by true glandular malfunctions. To eliminate that possibility—and that excuse—anyone who has a constant weight problem should have a thorough physical examination by a bariatrician, or doctor specializing in obesity.

Fat persons, however, do have a number of glandular and chemical abnormalities. In fact, anyone who has a substantial weight problem will often have abnormalities or at least values on the edges of normal in a number of lab or physical findings. Generally, though, these abnormal values develop as a result of the increased fat mass and are not themselves the cause of the excess weight.

Question: Is obesity more prevalent now than in the past? What about the painter Ruben's well-rounded women?

Answer: In the past, girth was evidence of worth. The poor were lucky to keep from starving, and the wealthy ostentatiously displayed their waistlines and their privileged status. Today, most Americans are financially able to select an adequate diet. Unfortunately, a paradox has emerged. Obesity in women is more likely to be seen in the lower socioeconomic groups than in the upper class. Only for men does the old adage hold true that the more a person can afford to eat, the more likely he is to be overweight. Affluence is less a factor today than is making wise choices about what to eat. To get ahead of the game, regardless of your income, learn more about nutrition and how to choose food wisely.

Question: Are Americans more overweight than people of other countries?

Answer: Such comparisons are very difficult to make on a worldwide scale, but Americans are certainly one of the three fattest nations, in spite of the billions of dollars spent on health care and diet products. Some nations, such as Italy or Greece, have a tradition of people putting on weight in middle age. Custom even sanctions it. Americans, on the other hand, have a fetish for slimness. Although aided by their traditions, such people as the Greeks lack our advantages in the fatness race—"advantages" such as unlimited calories from junk food and convenience foods, plus a sedentary culture that sends a 200-pound woman in a 3,000-pound automobile 500 yards to buy a 1-pound loaf of bread.

Question: What impact is the new interest in health, jogging, and exercise having on Americans' health?

Answer: Something positive is happening because for the first time the coronary death rate in young men is decreasing. No one is quite sure why this is happening, though, and recent nationwide tests by the President's Council on Physical Fitness have shown that the young are no more fit than they were ten years ago. The estimated percentage of obesity in the population has not changed, and every survey still reveals that a majority of Americans get *no* regular physical exercise. I hope the exercise craze will spread and prove durable, but from the evidence of patients coming into my office, most still have a long way to go.

Question: Why do people overeat and become fat?

Answer: There are so many reasons. Often obesity starts as a perceptual problem. From childhood, food is seen as the answer to a problem, or as a reward, or weapon, or tranquilizer, or it is not seen at all but is just mechanically eaten. Food is none of these things in reality. Food is made up of discrete items, each with a precise value in calories, vitamins, minerals, and fiber content. It may also be delicious, succulent, and nutritious, but until a person knows food for what it is, little progress can be made toward a permanent control of obesity. For example, the Fabulous Fructose Diet is based on using a particular type of simple sugar, fructose, and avoiding other types of carbohydrates that are absorbed into the blood stream as glucose. Weight loss on the diet and maintenance of that loss on the permanent eating plan depends on a diet high in protein, low in fat, and low in carbohydrates.

Still, a person who perceives cream-filled cupcakes as the answer to his problems of sexual frustration may fail at dieting. Ideally, while dieting you should simultaneously learn that cream-filled cupcakes help produce the undesirable glucose-insulin overreaction, that they don't really solve sexual problems or any other problems, and that most problems are solved by deciding what you want to happen and then working to make that occur. For dieting to have a permanent effect, behavior and motivation must also change.

Question: Why can't persons on the FFD drink caffeine or cola drinks in any quantity?

Answer: Caffeine is a stimulant that has some serious side effects when taken to excess. These include nervousness, irritability, insomnia, stomach or bowel upsets, headache, and rebound tiredness. Caffeine may exert what seems to be a good effect because of its ability to raise the blood sugar; however, a rebound, or reactive, type of low blood sugar can follow this high in about three to four hours. Unless more caffeine is consumed, the patient feels down, so usually a person with this type of caffeine addiction tends to drink caffeine-containing beverages all day long, producing the roller-coaster type of blood sugar curve that stimulates hunger when the lows occur.

Question: How much caffeine is in the beverages I drink?

Answer: In an 8-ounce glass or cup of the following beverages, there are the following amounts of caffeine or caffeinelike substances (all figures are in milligrams):

Brim Electric Perk	4.00
Brim Freeze-Dried Instant	2.70
Coca-Cola	32.00
Coffee (regular)	81.00

Diet Pepsi	24.00
Diet-Rite Cola	28.00
Doctor Pepper (all)	42.40
Nestlé's Decaf	0.24
Nestlé's Nescafé	9.36
Pepsi-Cola	24.00
Royal Crown Cola	28.00
Sanka	4.40
Tab	32.00
Taster's Choice Green Label	2.40
Tea (normal strength)	96.00

All these figures are approximate, and they can vary in the case of coffee or tea with the way they are prepared.

There is almost 400 times more caffeine in a cup of regular coffee as in a cup of Decaf. If you must drink coffee, try to have only one or two cups daily of regular and take the rest from decaffeinated brands.

Question: This diet is for the birds. I have another book that says I can stay healthy and lose 10 pounds a week indefinitely without dieting. How do you explain that?

Answer: This type of diet is, at best, a fraud and, at worst, dangerous to follow. A little arithmetic shows why, after the initial weight loss from the diuretic effect occurs, there is not that much actual fat loss.

A pound of fat in the body contains about 3,500 calories. A pound of muscle contains about 350 calories, partly because the muscle and organ tissues contain much more water and also because fat contains over twice as much energy per gram of dry weight as muscles does. This means that to lose a pound of fat, you have to have a deficit of 3,500 calories. A person who needs 2,000 calories a day to maintain his weight and only eats 1,000 will run a deficit of 1,000 calories a day, or 7,000 a week. This is two times 3,500, or two pounds of fat lost in a week.

If you go on one of the starvation or protein-wasting diets, you may need 2,000 calories a day and only take in 250, a deficit of 1,750 per day. After a period of adaptation, about half the calories will come from fat and half from valuable and needed protein that you cannot afford to lose. The deficit per day is 875 calories of fat and 875 of protein, or putting it in terms of pounds of weight loss, 875/3500 or ¼ pound of fat and 875/350, or 2½ pounds of vitally needed protein tissue per day. If full deficits are realized, the patient could lose over 19 pounds of weight in a week, but the results would eventually be fatal. Such diets are dangerous and unhealthy. A maximum deficit of 1,500 to 2,000 calories daily with the protein-sparing effect of the FFD is all you should realistically expect to achieve. Those who promise more are either dishonest or misinformed. They should be avoided for your own safety.

Question: Why does fructose play such an important part in these diets? Why not some other kind of sugar?

Answer: Fructose is important because of its biochemical and physical uniqueness. It is not absorbed as rapidly into the blood stream from the intestines as are the other simple sugars. Since fructose trickles into the blood stream and is absorbed into certain cells of the body without the need for insulin, there is no chance for the glucose-insulin roller coaster to develop, and dieting is easier. Several years ago, in a series of experiments, Dr. J. Daniel Palm showed that the use of fructose in small amounts could prevent the adrenalin surges that low blood sugar sets off, thus diminishing the stress response on the individual. Since the episodes of low blood sugar or stress from not eating cause many to fail at dieting, fructose is ideal because it helps to control these fluctuations.

Question: Is fructose new and experimental? Why haven't I heard of it before now?

Answer: Fructose is neither new nor experimental. Fructose is a natural sugar that has been identified and used for almost 100 years. It is a sugar found in many foods, such as apples or pears, commonly eaten by people. Until recently it was difficult and expensive to separate fructose from the other sugars it was combined with in these foods. In Europe, fructose has been used in the treatment of diabetes for years because it does not stimulate excess insulin production. Most of the world's production of pure fructose (by conversion from complex carbohydrates) is still carried out in Europe, although a half dozen companies are now entering the market in this country.

Question: Where can I get fructose-containing products?

Answer: Many of the companies listed in Appendix 6 have these products. We still are not as lucky as

Europeans, who produce a multitude of candies, confections, pastries, and beverages in which fructose is the sole sugar. Beware of any product that has fructose *and* another sugar (sucrose, dextrose, glucose, mannitol, sorbitol, xylitol, corn syrup, or others) added to the formula. Be sure that products you use contain only fructose. Do not buy something that says "high in fructose" or "enriched with fructose." These phrases are a dead giveaway that something else that you do not want is also present. Some of the soft drink companies are using a corn syrup with a slightly higher fructose content than they have used in the past. But these drinks still have a high sucrose and/or dextrose (glucose) content and should be avoided. The 90% fructose corn syrup is acceptable for up to half of your daily fructose ration.

Question: What benefits can I expect from exercising?

Answer: An obvious benefit is that you cannot eat when you are exercising. This point is not overlooked by experienced bariatricians. Anything that makes eating impractical is a boon to someone whose life is characterized by habitual munching.

Exercise can also change the entire chemical and enzymatic pattern of the body. With exercise, the body shifts chemical gears and reorganizes to burn energy more efficiently and rapidly. Over time, the oxygen-carrying capacity is enhanced, and tissues are supplied with life-giving oxygen in a more efficient manner. The adrenalin-hypoglycemia-stress cycle is short-circuited, and the internal environment of the body changes for the better. The result is a calmer person, better able to deal with the problems of life, including a reducing diet.

There is one more hidden benefit to exercise. When you exercise for twenty minutes or more every day, the entire level of the body's metabolism is raised slightly. This effect will persist for the next twenty-four hours and cause the body to burn extra energy even after the exercise is completed. The increase in metabolism will not burn a huge amount of extra fat every day, but as one dieter said, "I'll take any amount of fat loss any way I can get it."

Question: Won't I get hungrier if I exercise?

Answer: Contrary to popular belief, exercise functions as an appetite suppressant. It raises both the levels of fats and the glucose in the blood stream in a natural and healthy way, thus reducing hunger. Body sensors read these higher levels and you do not get messages that you are hungry. If you are about to suffer an attack of the nibbles, a brisk walk might be all you need to vanquish the feeling.

Question: Are all carbohydrates bad?

Answer: No responsible physician would say that carbohydrates are bad and should never be eaten. Carbohydrates, and particularly glucose, are essential to life. For some dieters, though, certain carbohydrates in the diet are detrimental. This occurs when carbohydrates cause low blood sugar.

Question: What exactly are carbohydrates?

Answer: The usual forms of carbohydates in our diets are sugars, starches, and complex carbohydrates, such as cellulose. The cellulose molecule, mostly found in raw vegetables, is not usually digestible by humans, and it only gives us energy when we cook it and thereby break it down by heat into smaller, more digestible particles. We get starches in vegetables and grains, with the two classic examples being the potato and wheat flour.

Sugars are either complex, usually having two molecules of simple sugars connected by a chemical bond, or simple. Human intestines can break the bonds between the complex sugars to convert them to simple sugar, and the simple sugar components are then absorbed into the blood stream.

Question: What are some of these sugars and their sources?

Answer: The common sugars are:

1. *Sucrose,* or table sugar, derived from cane, beets, or other sources. In the intestine, sucrose is split into equal halves of glucose and fructose, two of the three basic simple sugars.
2. *Lactose* is milk sugar. It is broken down into equal halves of glucose and galactose, the third simple sugar.
3. *Glucose* is the primary energy fuel for the brain. It is rapidly absorbed by the small intestine and enters the blood stream faster than all other sugars do. Humans are able to form glucose from fructose and galactose, and vice versa. When a new mother is producing breast milk, her body takes glucose, changes it to galactose, hooks it to another molecule of glucose to form lactose, a prime component of mother's milk. Glucose is also obtained from the digestion of starches and similar foods. The common denom-

inator of all of these sugars (sucrose, lactose, maltose, fructose, and galactose) is their final conversion by the liver and other body structures to glucose and the subsequent conversion of this substance into energy, either active or stored.

4. *Maltose,* derived from plant sources, is formed from two glucose molecules that join together and then split to again yield the same two glucoses when they are needed by the body.

5. *Fructose* is a sugar contained in a number of plants. Its structure and utilization in the body differs markedly from that of other sugars. Fructose is absorbed in a much less active way by the small intestine and trickles into the blood stream more slowly. It should be pointed out here that the behavior of fructose when taken alone and that of fructose taken with other sugars is markedly different. It is a shame, but many earlier faulty studies done with fructose and other sugars are still cited as proof that fructose does not work. When these experiments are repeated using fructose alone, the results are quite different. New, updated references are given in the bibliography.

Question: Sugar is sugar as far as I am concerned. Why is fructose any better than glucose or table sugar? Won't I get fat if I eat sugar?

Answer: Any sugar will make you fat if it, plus the other foods you eat, add up to more calories than you burn. The problem with most sugars is that they stimulate the production of excess insulin, thus causing the glucose-insulin trap described earlier in this book.

Unlike glucose, fructose is absorbed directly by the cells without the help of insulin. Even in large amounts, fructose does not result in a flood of insulin, followed by hypoglycemia and hunger. This is especially critical if your weight problem is linked to a glucose-insulin roller-coaster ride every day.

Once inside the cell, fructose takes the common pathway used in the burning of all sugars and is converted either into energy, if calories are needed, or into fat, if they are not. For this reason, the daily allowance of fructose must be small, and it must be combined with a total number of calories that will produce a caloric deficit and weight loss each day. Under deficit conditions, there is little likelihood that excess body fat will be produced. An intake of more than 100 grams of fructose daily is not recommended.

Question: I have been on the Atkins diet and lost weight and later regained it. Why don't you recommend this type of diet?

Answer: For some of my patients I do use a modification of this diet. I tend to steer away from that type of diet, however, because of the high fat content. The main reason I do not use it now is the better track record for sustained weight loss that the Fabulous Fructose Diet shows.

Question: Won't drinking all this water make me heavier?

Answer: Fat makes you overweight; water doesn't. Temporary bloating with fluids is related to your body's salt content and not specifically to water. Contradictory as this may seem, when you are loaded with excess fluid, drinking more water helps you get rid of the unwanted edema.

Question: I get upset when I diet strenuously and then get on the scale and haven't lost any weight. What is going on when that happens?

Answer: When the body burns a pound of fat, a little over a pound of water is produced from the chemical breakdown of the fat. If that water is temporarily held in the body, the result could be a slight weight gain, resulting in disgust and possible problem eating. The scales are pitiless—they weigh a pound of water the same as a pound of fat. What is needed is an attitude of persistence, coupled with massive amounts of water intake. The final, desired result will be the loss of the extra fluid and further progress.

Question: Is any one type of water better for drinking?

Answer: Drink whatever water you like, as long as you are comfortable with it. Regular tap water is all right in most localities. Bottled mineral waters or distilled water are preferred by some, and you may want to try them. Bottled spring water also has an excellent taste. Whatever you choose, drink lots!

Question: Is it true that grapefruit juice and cider vinegar have a special fat-burning effect?

Answer: If you believe that one, I have some uranium stocks, Confederate bonds, and a few bridges I would like to sell you. Both of these liquids have certain valuable minerals and are included as part of the Permanent Diet for that reason, but they have no special fat-melting effects. In fact, a common misconception is that grapefruit juice has no calories. Not so! Unsweetened grapefruit juice has 48 calories in one-half cup, compared to unsweetened orange juice, which has an average of 56 calories for the same quantity. Fruit juices are an excellent source of nutrients, but they have no place on any of the FFD systems until the Permanent Diet is begun.

Question: Can I have my nightly cocktail on this diet?

Answer: Have all the water you want—just don't mix any alcohol with it. The purpose of the Fabulous Fructose Diet is to get you to target weight as quickly as possible. Alcohol sabotages a diet in three ways. First, it can totally wreck your fat-burning machinery. Second, it provides a large number of concentrated calories. Finally, it can aggravate a low blood sugar condition and make you feel rotten, along with producing increased hunger.

Question: Will I ever get to drink alcohol again?

Answer: On the Permanent Diet you will be permitted a certain number of fat shares daily. Alcohol can be counted as a fat. The following list is a guide to substituting certain kinds and amounts of alcoholic beverages for fat shares.

Conversion of Fat Shares to Alcohol Equivalents
One fat share equals any one of the following:
1. ⅔ ounce * of distilled spirits (bourbon, gin, rum, rye, Scotch, vodka)
2. 3 fluid ounces of beer
3. 4 fluid ounces of ale
4. 2 fluid ounces of champagne

* One fluid ounce is approximately 30 milliliters.

5. 1⅔ ounces of dry white or red wine
6. 1⅓ ounces of sweet wine

Question: When I go on a diet, I feel deprived and depressed. Is this normal?

Answer: Yes. Food is cheap, always available, and it never talks back. Consequently, many obese persons tend to use it as a shield against the world. It becomes a psychological crutch. The idea of being cut off from food becomes vaguely threatening and can cause depression. Also, many obese persons have a flat glucose-tolerance curve and are usually a little starved for energy. Erroneously, but in an attempt to raise the amount of glucose available for the brain and body, they eat constantly. Fructose will solve this problem by making energy available in a form that does not trigger the insulin overreaction. Some time is required for the psychological dependence to be overcome, and that is what the mental exercises in this book are designed to help with.

Question: What about suits that cause dieters to sweat off pounds, or belts that are worn to slim the waist?

Answer: Slimming sweat suits and special belts are an excellent lesson in consumer education. In this case, the seller gets your money, and you get the lesson. The lesson is that sweating, with water and salt loss, is not a method of taking off fat. In addition, there are no miracle exercise machines, baths, jellies, or rubs that can make the fat flee from your hips or other trouble spots. As an example, one study showed that tennis players had just as much fat on the racquet arm, which they exercised for hours a day, as they had on the nonexercised arm. Sit-ups and leg raises are beautiful for tightening sagging muscles, but a bay window can only be trimmed by burning the fat.

By combining abdominal muscle exercises with a reducing diet, you will have the most efficient reducing program possible. Improved muscle tone will flatten your silhouette at the same time that fat cells are shrinking due to the decrease in stored fat. As a helpful point for consumers who use exercise machines, no one has ever shown that a decrease in stored fat resulted from machines that knead, shake, or pummel the flesh. By all means, use these machines if you like the feeling they give, but plan your improvement program around walking and simple muscle-tightening exercises.

Question: Do Americans really eat a lot of sugar, or is this just another rumor?

Answer: Americans eat an average of 112 pounds of table sugar per person per year. This average includes men, women, and children. Some people eat almost none, and others take in a massive amount every day of their lives. This is a change from earlier times when our only source of sweetness was honey and fruits. Not until the early 1800s did sugar become less than a luxury item. It is said that in colonial houses the silver was often left out, while the sugar was always kept in a locked container.

Question: Why the emphasis on fresh fruits and vegetables and unprocessed meats?

Answer: Many processed food items are attractively packaged and backed by billions of dollars in promotion, packaging, and advertising. In most cases, though, the vitamin and mineral content of these products has been decreased markedly by food processing. To help their anemic taste they are too often loaded with salt and sugar. Some of today's foods taste great, but they are empty calories, devoid of other nutritive value. Small wonder that it is so easy to gain weight.

Question: Can I inherit obesity from my parents?

Answer: Heredity and environment may be powerful influences. A child with two obese parents has an 80 percent chance of becoming obese as an adult. Interesting studies of twins raised in different homes have attempted to determine if the child becomes fat because of environment or heredity. Results are still inconclusive, although it is fairly well established that in infancy, overfeeding may lead to an increase in the number of fat cells. Such an increase in fat cells may well increase insulin requirements and lead to a lifelong tendency to store fat in excessive quantities.

This may be an ominous portent for the future. Millions of young people today have obese parents, a disadvantage that their parents did not have. Overweight parents may find this thought an extra incentive to help in their struggle to lose weight.

Question: Has the American diet changed in terms of protein and carbohydrate content from that of past generations?

Answer: U.S. Department of Agriculture figures show a continuous decline in the amount of vegetables eaten, even though they are available year round instead of seasonally as they were in the past. While the amount of protein in the diet has not changed much in the past thirty years, the amount of fat has climbed from providing just over 20 percent of the calories in the average diet to providing over 40 percent. This means that the contribution of carbohydrates has shrunk by almost a third.

Much of the carbohydrate contribution now comes from sugar, so it is obvious that the average American gets most of his energy requirements in the form of glucose-producing sugars or starches plus high-calorie fats. An ounce of fat contains more than twice as many calories as an ounce of either carbohydrate or protein. Restaurant industry figures show that an increasing number of meals are eaten out. As a rule restaurant meals tend to be higher in fat, so the trend toward higher fat consumption comes from that new source, too.

Question: Is modern life with all its stresses responsible for the increased obesity of Americans?

Answer: The emotional stress of living in a modern urban civilization may be no worse than that of being a farmer in the last century, but no one has proven it yet. Our great-grandparents had to contend with disease, crop failure, fire, recessions, and the Civil War. Today we have noise, pollution, cancer, heart disease, the bomb, changing life-styles, sexual-identity problems, and television. Whether life is harder on the nerves today than it was a hundred years ago is a moot point, since the past is out of reach, but one indication of the toll emotional stress does take is the fact that emotional disturbances hospitalize or disable more persons than do cancer and heart disease combined. The odds that a person will need psychiatric care sometime in his or his life are one in eight. Problems in dealing with people and life situations are major contributors to the masses of unwanted poundage that I see every year on my patients. This is particularly true with binge eaters, who gorge them-themselves with incredible amounts of food on an irregular basis. The solution to such problems lies in learning new ways to deal with such stresses. Some methods for handling stress were discussed in Chapter 4.

Question: Can I have a little treat on these diets, such as a small piece of pie or cake?

Answer: No. There are some special treats on a few of the diets, but pie and cake are not among them. On the Meals-and Munch Diet, fruit is included as a treat, and on the Dependable Diet, a special type of cheesecake or cannoli made with fructose is permitted. The other diets are deliberately designed to steer you away from being rewarded by your taste buds and into being rewarded by a steadily diminishing waistline.

Question: Are low-calorie diets dangerous?

Answer: They can be. With proper medical supervision and the inclusion of adequate protein and other nutrients, very low calorie diets can be continued safely for many months. To simply decide that you are going to fast or go on a low-calorie diet without knowing what you are doing is an entirely different and dangerous matter. Prolonged and unsupervised fasting is extremely dangerous and can result in death. The human metabolism is a very carefully balanced process that requires the constant intake of many essential substances. Programs such as the FFD are carefully worked out to supply these needs. With proper monitoring, there has never yet been a serious illness or death on such a program.

On the other hand there are cases in which people who casually made up their own programs or who followed unsound programs, such as rice diets and other unbalanced diets, have died. Your future health and happiness are based on your nutrient intake, so do not play around with diets that promise magic and ignore sound nutrition.

Question: On the fructose diet systems, can I go out to eat?

Answer: Yes, it is possible to eat out on all these systems. Simply order something that fits into the diet. The Vegetarian Fructose Diet may be a problem, but you can have a salad, and you should supply your own dressing. Restaurant-sized portions are normally twice the size of protein portions in the diets and may have unwanted extra calories added in gravy or sauces. Learn to judge the size of portions before you venture out without your scale. Only broiled food should be ordered, and that without sauces or gravy. A starchy side dish (potatoes, peas, or rice) will often be included with the meal even if you don't order it. Don't eat it. Naturally, sauces, and all salad dressings except a light oil and vinegar must be omitted. Most restaurant-prepared vegetables are taboo unless you ask for boiled or steamed vegetables without butter or margarine. Drink unsweetened, diluted ice tea, water, or decaffeinated coffee. Club soda with a slice of lemon or a sugar-free soda will give you something to drink when your friends are having their alcoholic beverages.

Studies of people with weight problems show that obese persons are extremely responsive to food cues. Keeping these cues to a minimum will help you control your life and your weight, so think twice before treating yourself to a restaurant meal early in your diet.

Question: Is a fructose diet expensive?

Answer: No, it is not. In fact, the average person will find that he can follow the FFD for less than it costs to eat in his or her usual way. On the Fabulous Fructose Diet, less food is bought than before. And since the food is fresh and unprocessed, it will be cheaper than packaged food. Additional vitamins, minerals, potassium, and fructose will be new expenses, but their cost will be spread over a number of days or weeks. In addition to spending less on food, you will be improving your health, a priceless commodity.

A variable item in your expenses will be the doctor's charges, depending on what type of tests are run and how closely you need to be supervised. Naturally, the charges for weekly monitoring will be higher than checking in and weighing once every six weeks. Depending on your age, physical condition, and the date of your last physical examination, your doctor may suggest a complete physical prior to starting on one of the programs. Charges for this vary, but are worth the money in terms of benefit to your health and peace of mind.

Question: A friend of mine was on amphetamines and lost her appetite entirely. Why should I fool around with the FFD when I can lose without dieting?

Answer: Some of these appetite-suppressing drugs do cause a rapid initial weight loss. There is no way, however, to sustain the loss, and there are some potentially serious effects with this type of medicine. I do not normally prescribe these drugs, although there are certain limited cases when they are useful for a time. Drugs based on the amphetamine formula can blunt the appetite, but the effect is short-lived and is often followed by a return of lost weight and hunger when the drug is discontinued. Often the patient winds up heavier than before the diet. These drugs also have side effects that include headache, insomnia, nervousness, and physical and psychological dependence.

Question: What about water pills?

Answer: Diuretics are drugs that cause a loss of body water and consequently a temporary loss of weight, but not a loss of fat. Body fat is unaffected, but there is a loss of potassium, magnesium, and other substances needed by the body. The Fabulous Fructose Diet has its own natural and mild diuretic effect without these synthetic medications.

Question: Why is it that my husband and I eat the same foods; but he stays the same weight, and I have to fight to keep my weight down?

Answer: Men have a larger body size and greater muscle mass. Both of these contribute to a higher caloric need, which means that large persons can eat more before it goes into fat storage. When they diet, they burn fat at a more rapid rate. A woman's hormonal make-up also keeps her from losing as rapidly. Her principal hormone is estrogen, which tends to encourage water retention and may retard fat utilization. A man's major hormone is testosterone, a powerful fat mobilizer and stimulator of protein building. There is also a cultural bias operating here. Women are generally more concerned with buying and preparing food than are men. Many women's magazines focus on food. In addition, there are undoubtedly factors in the socialization of women that guide them to respond to conflict passively—for example, by eating—rather than aggressively and assertively. Appendix 10 contains material to help you combat this socialization.

Question: How much exercise is necessary?

Answer: This is covered in Chapter 6, but at the risk of being repetitious, let's mention a few facts. You do not have to run a marathon or chop wood for an hour to get the calorie-burning benefits of exercise. Any activity you do burns up *some* energy. The only question is, how much energy do you want to burn and how quickly? Walking is excellent, requires no special equipment, is cheap and effective. Walking briskly for an hour every day will burn enough extra energy to give the average-sized person a 36-pound weight loss in a year. The beauty of exercise is that the heavier a person is, the more energy he can burn in movement.

Walking is excellent exercise. If it has been years since you did anything more vigorous than opening a pack of potato chips, you should begin by walking a few hundred yards a day. Do it religiously every day, and about every third day, extend the distance by 50 to 100 yards. Gradually extend your walking until you are walking at least 20 to 30 minutes a day. The speed should be the same as if you were walking home in a cold, windy rainstorm with no coat and a very full bladder. Keeping that image in mind will give you an idea of how briskly you should be walking.

Proper shoes are also an essential aid to an effective walking program. Many stores sell shoes for running and walking. Tell the clerk you are a walker and let him suggest the proper fit and design.

Any activity that raises your energy expenditure will help. Do housework, garden, walk up and down stairs, or walk from the farthest part of a parking lot —anything helps. The point to remember is that exercise is not something only an athlete can do. A walking program and other activities are well within the reach of everyone; and they work.

Appendix 1

GLUCOSE-INSULIN TRAP

A GLUCOSE-TOLERANCE test (GTT), which is a simple blood test performed in a doctor's office, measures one's reaction to and tolerance for sugar. Figure 1 shows the three patterns that commonly occur: normal, diabetic (or excessive glucose); and hypoglycemic (or low blood sugar). The hypoglycemic pattern is the one that most frequently appears in persons who are overweight and unable to diet.

Figure 2 shows the four different types of hypoglycemia. One kind (S) is indicative of someone who has had stomach surgery and need only be of interest to a doctor treating such a person. In a sense, it is an artificially induced hypoglycemic curve. (B) represents the borderline diabetic, who requires medical supervision. The (P) and (F) curves are the kind most commonly found in persons with diet problems.

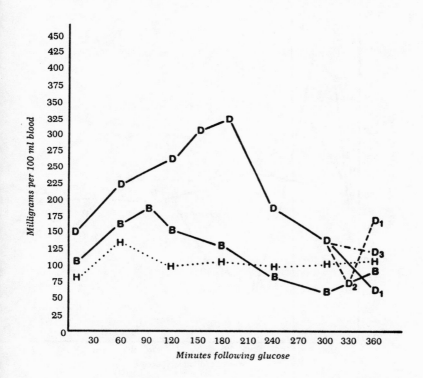

Figure 1. (H) is the diagram of a normal healthy person's GTT, (B) is that of a mild or borderline diabetic, and (D) is that of a severe diabetic. The (H) curve is normal as described, but the borderline diabetic (B) has a slightly elevated curve and may or may not have a hypoglycemic "tail" near the end of the test. The severe diabetic (D) has a delayed, high peak and then can either stay higher than normal (D3), have a terminal hypoglycemic tail (D1), or show hypoglycemic and then rebound with a secondary peak (D2).

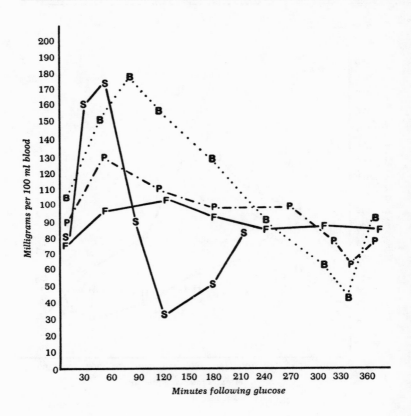

Figure 2. The four different types of possible hypoglycemia curves are diagramed above. (S) represents someone who has had stomach sugery, with a high, early peak and rapid drop. The test stopped after 3½ hours. (B) again represents the borderline diabetic with a hypoglycemia tail at the end. (P) represents the pseudohypoglycemia, with an essentially normal curve until the last few hours. (F) curve shows the classical "flat curve" picture seen in many dietary failures, particularly those with little energy and an inability to stay on any diet for long.

Persons who show signs of hypoglycemia may have any combination of symptoms. All symptoms do not appear in one person, and individual patterns vary greatly. When excessive amounts of epinephrine are being released, the following symptoms may appear:

> rapid heart rate
> irritability
> restlessness
> anxiety
> insomnia
> indigestion
> cold feet and hands
> dry or cottony mouth
> nervousness

Symptoms that are likely to be present when there is a drop in the glucose supply to the brain are:

> mental confusion
> faintness or dizziness
> lack of concentration
> uncontrollable hunger
> exhaustion

Appendix 2

GLUCOSE REACTION IN
THE HUMAN BODY

Figure 3 (opposite) shows how the human body reacts to glucose. Further explanation of this highly complicated process is provided in the material below.

Figure 3 (opposite). This demonstrates the alarm reaction following (1) a drop in the blood glucose levels. Sensors (2) pick up the drop in glucose and funnel the alarm reaction through the brain centers that control this glucose level (3). Various target glands (4) are stimulated. In one way or another they produce an elevation in the concentration of glucose leaving the liver (5), producing (6) an elevation in the concentration of glucose in the blood. Sensors (7) pick up this increased concentration and (8) cut off the alarm reaction. This is obviously an oversimplification of a very complex process, but serves the purpose of showing the basic way this intricate system works to maintain a steady level of glucose for the energy needs of the brain and central nervous system.

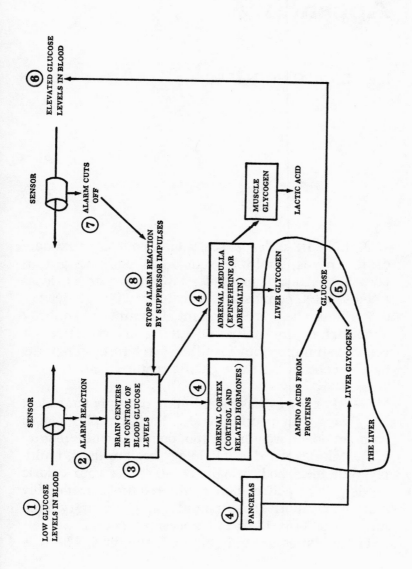

Appendix 3

BASAL CALORIC NEEDS

WOMEN In order to calculate your approximate caloric needs, multiply your ideal body weight in pounds by 16. For example, a woman with an ideal weight of 100 pounds would require 1,600 calories per day unless she were pregnant, lactating, chemically abnormal, or unusually underactive or overactive. Or you can multiply your ideal body weight in kilograms by 35 to obtain the same caloric requirement.

MEN For the average-sized man, multiply your ideal body weight in pounds by 18. For example, a man with an ideal weight of 150 pounds would require 2,700 calories per day. (If kilograms are used, multiply your ideal body weight by 40 to get your caloric needs.) Very active men might require considerably more (25 calories per pound) and sedentary men might need only 13 or 14 calories per pound.

These figures are only approximate ones. The true

test of a maintenance diet is whether a daily level of caloric intake will maintain the body weight within a certain tolerable limit over a period of months and years. Figures are for mature men and women in good health and in the age groups of 25 to 35. Older and younger persons will have slightly different requirements, but these figures will be close enough for the majority of those trying the FFD.

SOURCE: Health and Welfare Canada. Reproduced by permission of the Minister of Supply and Services Canada.

Appendix 4

THE MILKSHAKE DIET

THE NIOFAST is probably the most effective and rapid weight-loss diet available; but because of its severely restricted caloric intake, it must be taken under the supervision of a doctor, preferably a bariatrician. Courses on the use of NIOFast, also referred to as the Milkshake Diet, are held approximately three times a year across the United States and Canada by the Weight Control Research Institute. Dates and places can be obtained by writing to:

    The Weight Control Research Institute
    Suite 300
    2480 Windy Hill Road
    Marietta, Georgia 30067
    Tel. (404) 952-7681

Appendix 5

RECIPES FOR FABULOUS
FRUCTOSE DIETS

Cooper's Cannoli

2 pounds ricotta cheese
¼ pound fructose
⅛ pound carob chips
2 tablespoons pistachio nuts, chopped
8 cannoli shells

Place ricotta in cheesecloth and squeeze to remove excess moisture. Combine all ingredients, except the cannoli shells, in a blender. Blend on low speed until creamy. Fill cannoli shells. Chill before serving. Serves 8.

Cooper's Cheesecake

1 pound ricotta cheese
2 eight-ounce packages cream cheese
⅓ cup fructose granules
4 eggs
1 tablespoon lemon juice
2 teaspoons vanilla extract
1 stick butter (¼ pound), melted
1 pint sour cream

Preheat oven to 325° F. Cream the ricotta cheese and squeeze in cheesecloth to remove excess moisture. Place in large mixing bowl. Mix in the cream cheese and fructose granules. Add 1 egg at a time and slowly blend until all eggs are mixed in. Stir in lemon juice and vanilla extract. Add one-fourth pound melted butter to mixture—mix well. Fold in the sour cream; stir until smooth. Bake in oven for 1 hour and 10 minutes. Turn off oven and let cheesecake rest in it for 2 hours; do not open door. For best results use a cheese cake pan.

Diet Yogurt

½ cup plain yogurt
1 rounded teaspoon fructose-containing jam,
    jelly, or preserves (See Appendix 6.)
1 serving fruit, as permitted on your diet plan

Combine all ingredients and mix well.

Sour Cream Pudding

8 ounces cottage cheese
18 grams granulated fructose
½ cup sour cream
fruit for garnish

*Place cottage cheese and 15 grams of the fructose in
the blender and blend until smooth. Add sour cream
and blend again, until smooth. Divide the mixture
into two custard cups; top with fruit if desired and
glaze with remaining fructose. Chill before serving.*

Dr. Palm's Never-Fail Fructose Fudge

2 cups (1 pound) fructose granules
1 ounce baking chocolate
2 ounces cream cheese
¼ teaspoon vanilla
1 tablespoon butter
pinch of salt

*Powder the fructose in a blender, half a cup at a time,
run at high speed. Melt the cream cheese, butter, and
½ cup of the powdered fructose over low heat. Remove from the heat and add the vanilla and salt.*

Allow mixture to cool for a few minutes. Add the remaining powdered fructose. Knead mixture until smooth. Press out on buttered cookie sheet, score and allow to dry. Store in closed container. Substitute ½ teaspoon of Kool-Aid powder for the chocolate for a new taste treat.

Dr. Palm's Swedish Cheesecake
Developed by J. Daniel Palm, Ph.D.

2 eggs
3 tablespoons water
12 ounces creamed, low-fat cottage cheese
⅓ cup fructose syrup
1 teaspoon vanilla
3 tablespoons dry skim milk
1 teaspoon flour

Beat eggs well. Beat in other ingredients, one by one, by hand or in a blender. If using a blender, fold in the cottage cheese by hand to give a chewy consistency to the cheesecake. Bake in 8″ by 8″ pan or medium-sized casserole 55 minutes at 350°.

Kool-Aid-like Beverage
This drink may be used instead of the French Lemonade at mid-morning and after dinner. Any powdered, sugar-free beverage that contains no more than four calories per eight-ounce serving is fine. There are multiple flavors, including lemonade, available. To an eight-ounce portion add nine grams of fructose. This is the amount in three packets of the granulated fruc-

*tose, or in 1½ teaspoons of Fructose90 syrup. Stir well
and add ice.*

Flounder-Fromage Fillet

2 ounces diet French dressing
5½-ounce flounder fillet (raw weight)
1 tablespoon grated cheese

*Brush the French dressing all over the fillet and fol-
low with grated cheese until the fillet is covered with
the cheese on both sides. Sprinkle with paprika, salt
and pepper. Bake in non-stick pan in oven at high
temperature for about twelve minutes. Serve with
garnish of parsley and sprinkle lemon or lime juice
to taste.*

Orange Delight Salad Dressing

Two tablespoons vinegar
One tablespoon oil, safflower preferred, but
    any will do
Two ounces orange flavored liquid protein

*Mix and use on salads in the amount of three table-
spoons or less per salad. It is particularly good on raw
spinach salads. If larger amounts are desired, simply
keep the proportions of the three ingredients the same.*

Vinaigrette Salad Dressing

Two ounces safflower oil
Two ounces wine vinegar
Three ounces water
Three ounces Chianti or dry Burgundy

Three grams fructose granules
½ teaspoon garlic salt
¼ chopped dill pickle
One teaspoon chopped chives
dash of cayenne pepper
One teaspoon capers

Mix and use on salads in the amount of three table-spoons or less per salad. If taste is too strong you can add water to taste.

Vinegar and Oil Salad Dressing
Three ounces safflower oil or other vegetable
    oil
Nine ounces vinegar

Mix together in shake container. Shake before each use, using up to three tablespoons on each salad. Salt, pepper and other spices may be added to taste.

Other Salad Dressings Permitted
You may use any diet salad dressing that contains no more than six calories per tablespoon. Up to three tablespoons of this type of dressing may be used on each salad. BE A LABEL-READER AND CHECK THE NUMBER OF CALORIES ON THE LABEL BEFORE BUYING!

Instructions for Preparation of Scallops
Seven ounces of fresh or frozen scallops,
    drained and patted dry
One tablespoon melted margarine

Take the scallops and carefully coat them by dipping in the melted margarine until all sides are covered.

Place on flat, non-stick baking surface and broil at high heat for about two minutes each side. Place salt, pepper, and butter-flavored salt on both sides. Makes five ounces of cooked weight, equal to two protein shares.

Spring Garden Salad

Make a salad with green peppers, mushrooms, bean sprouts, celery bits and low-calorie Italian dressing. Try and use freshly sprouted bean sprouts if possible. Each salad is one loosely-packed measuring cup.

Sea Food Dip (Butter-Wine Dip or Meat Sauce)

For dipping shrimp, scallops and other sea food to enhance the flavor. Take one teaspoon of melted margarine or butter and combine with one teaspoon white dry wine, salt and pepper to taste and either ½ teaspoon of Worcestershire or 1 teaspoon of soy sauce. Stir until thoroughly mixed and use as a dip or as a brushed-on flavor enhancer.

Butterworth Omelet

Beat one egg in small bowl with three ounces ground beef that has been previously cooked and drained well. Stir until thoroughly mixed and the ground beef particles are well distributed throughout the egg. Cook in pan with ½ teaspoon oil added. Makes an omelet with two protein shares.

Stuffed Green Pepper

Remove the top of a large green pepper and scoop out the inner contents. Take four ounces cooked ground beef that has been well drained and add to it 1 table-

*spoon chopped onion, a pinch of dry thyme, a pinch
of salt and pepper, ¼ teaspoon lemon juice, a pinch
of garlic salt and one teaspoon tomato juice. Blend
well and place inside the pepper. Bake at about 360°
for 25 minutes.*

Chicken Liver Omelet
2 ounces (raw weight) chicken livers,
　　chopped
1 teaspoon chopped onion (optional)
2 lightly beaten eggs

*Into a non-stick pan add 1 teaspoon oil. Lightly brown
the chopped liver and onions over moderate heat for
about three minutes. Add the two eggs and scramble
until the desired consistency is reached. Makes a two-
share serving.*

Stuffed Flank Steak
*From M. Summerour and S. Corriher of
Rich's Cooking School, Atlanta*
1 cup finely chopped celery
¼ cup finely chopped onion
1 cup finely chopped mushrooms
½ teaspoon thyme
1 sixteen-ounce raw flank steak
Sauce:
2 tablespoons BV (bottled beef extract)
1 lemon, juiced
1 clove garlic, crushed
1 tablespoon corn or safflower oil

*Spray a non-stick pan with vegetable oil spray. Com-
bine all ingredients for stuffing and saute lightly. In*

the meantime, make a pocket in the steak. After sauteing stuffing, loosely pack it into the pocket of the steak. Close side of steak with toothpicks.

Combine sauce ingredients in a bowl. Place steak in a baking dish. Brush with sauce. Broil approximately six minutes on each side, varying according to thickness of steak. Brush frequently with sauce during broiling time. Place steak on a serving platter, pour remainder of sauce over meat. Slice on the diagonal. Makes 12 ounces cooked weight of flank steak, with each four-ounce portion being two protein shares.

French Lemonade

Combine 6½ ounces of Perrier or similar sparkling-water beverage with the juice of ½ lemon or lime and nine grams fructose (three packets of 3 grams, or 1½ teaspoons of the fructose90 syrup). Shake vigorously or blend and add ice.

Paddington's Quiche

8 one-ounce slices of Mozzarella cheese
    (legal only with quiche)
6 beaten eggs
½ cup plain, unsweetened yogurt (also
    legal only with quiche)
½ teaspoon salt
12 ounces boiled shrimp or ten ounces
    chopped lean ham or 10 ounces
    ground beef (precooked and chopped
    into small fragments)

Preheat oven to 375°. Line a round pie pan or quiche pan evenly with the eight slices of Mozza-

rella cheese to make the "crust" for the quiche. Take the six beaten eggs and combine in a bowl with yogurt and salt. Mix well and pour into pan. Sprinkle the shrimp, ham, or ground beef evenly into mixture in pan. Garnish with a small amount of chopped green peppers, celery, or raw mushrooms if desired. Bake for 25 minutes in preheated oven. Remove from heat and let stand at least five minutes before serving. Cut into six wedges. Each of the six wedges contains two shares.

Tuna (or Salmon) Crispies

6 ounces water-packed tuna or salmon,
    drained well
¼ cup finely chopped celery
1 beaten egg (optional, but desirable)
Salt and/or onion salt to taste
2 teaspoons Worcestershire sauce

Mix all ingredients in bowl until texture is even. Shape into two equal patties. Fry in moderately hot non-stick skillet until crispy brown on both sides. Each Crispie patty contains one protein share.

Appendix 6

ADVICE ON BUYING
FRUCTOSE PRODUCTS

ALTHOUGH FRUCTOSE is used to supplement many foods—dietetic and otherwise—pure fructose products are not common. Finding them often requires careful reading of labels and of product information.

It is important, however, to find these products because fructose loses its advantages when combined with other sugars. Therefore, if a label says "high in fructose" or "enriched with fructose" do not buy it. Also be careful of products that contain a mixture of fructose and protein, along with other food items.

Soft drinks now contain a syrup that is 55 percent fructose, but this amount is too low to be a true fructose product. Never use a product like this with less than a 90 percent fructose content.

The most economical way to buy fructose is in chewable tables or in premeasured packets. Always buy it in the pure form without additives or other food products. One exception is the premeasured packets of casein-lactalbumin-fructose, but these are only available through a doctor.

Appendix 7

THIS LIST of suppliers of fructose products is not intended to be complete. It is a list of suppliers of acceptable products known to the author at the time of the writing of this book. In addition, no endorsement of any of these companies and their products is intended.

When writing these companies, enclose a stamped, self-addressed envelope and request any information they may have. Some will send you catalogs, and others publish recipe booklets showing how to use their products.

Suppliers of Fructose Products

Batter-Lite Foods, Inc.
P.O. Box 476
Beloit, Wisconsin 53511 (M–D) (G–T–CM–J–B)

Control Drug, Inc.
230 Boiling Springs Avenue
East Rutherford, New Jersey 07073
Sales to doctors only
1-800-631-8373 (T)

Doctor's Choice-Healthmart
1416 Seventh Avenue
Beaver Falls, Pennsylvania 15010 (M–D) (G–T–J–S)

Earthquest Ltd.
3100 Maple Drive
Atlanta, Georgia 30305 (M) (FP)

General Nutrition Corporation
921 Penn Avenue
Pittsburgh, Pennsylvania 15230 (M–D) (G–S–T)

Lanpar-Parmae Co.
Sales to doctors only (FP)
1-800-527-9425

Miller Pharmaceutical Co.
Sales to doctors only
1-800-323-2935 (T–FP)

North Nassau Dispensary
1691 Northern Boulevard
Manhasset, New York 11030 (G)

Pfanstiehl Laboratories, Inc.
1219 Glen Rock Avenue
Waukegan, Illinois 60085 (M–D) (T)

Sanavita Corp.
Suite 1006
575 Madison Avenue
New York, New York 10022 (M) (T–J) (B)

Vitose Corp.
154 Burlington
P.O. Drawer D
Clarendon Hills, Illinois 60514 (D) (T)

C. G. Whitlock Process Co.
P.O. Box 259
Springfield, Illinois 62705 (S)

Codes for fructose products.
M direct mail sales to consumers
G granules in packets, premeasured
CM cake and cookie mixes with fructose
S fructose syrup, bulk or packaged
D sold in stores
T chewable tablets
J jams, jellies, and preserves
B cookbook
FP fructose and protein formula

Appendix 8

BEWARE THE FEEDER

DURING THE HOLIDAY SEASONS, and for that matter any time of year, you must be on the lookout for a vicious creature that preys on dieters, *the feeder*. They come in all shapes, sizes, and ages, but they have one common characteristic—they will try to wreck your diet.

Their motivations differ, but the results are the same—another diet down the drain. The purpose of this note is to make you aware that feeders exist, of some of their reasons for ruining your diet, and of how you can deal with them.

Feeders are more likely to be female, although there are some male feeders. The thin feeder is either normal weight or slightly overweight. The presence of someone fat makes this person look thinner. If a fat friend starts losing weight, a little bit of jealousy comes into the picture, and this feeder is apt to try to sabotage the dieter's efforts to lose.

The fat feeder may have several reasons for feeding you. She may not want you to look better than she does, or she may miss you as an eating buddy. She usually will not go to an ice cream parlor or a restaurant specializing in starchy foods unless she can go with a group of people. It is not as embarrassing to overeat if you are in a group. All of a sudden you no longer want to go to those places, and it makes her uncomfortable. The result is that she will try to tempt you to get back into her group of overeaters.

The last type of feeder is the grandparent figure. He or she may not be a grandparent, but the motivation is the same. This is a person who shows love by feeding someone. Anyone who doesn't accept this "love" by eating what is offered makes this feeder uncomfortable, to the point where she/he will almost demand that you go off your diet to please her/him.

All three types of feeders use the same tactics, some direct and some very subtle. Inviting you for dinner and then having nothing you can eat without going off your diet is a favorite trick, as is having you for a bridge game and pointedly placing a plate of dessert in front of you without giving you a chance to refuse. A good tactic is to tell a feeder in advance that you can only eat special foods and that you would like to bring your own supplies with you. The understanding friend will go along with this and accept that you are on a rigid diet. Never let yourself be caught away from home at the mercy of a feeder. Refuse invitations if known feeders are involved.

You don't have to be a social outcast, but certain environmental influences are deadly to a diet. A good idea is to stay away from church suppers, banquets, family reunions, and holiday parties unless you can bring your own supply of food. If this is impossible, then attend the function after the food is served or leave before the food is served if the food is the last thing on the program.

One favorite tactic of feeders is to remark how bad, how wrinkled, how much older, or even how good you look. The remark is then followed by their saying that you don't need to lose any more weight. One good response is to say, "What is your purpose in telling me this?" A feeder usually will be unable to answer, or she/he may say that she/he is just concerned about you. If she/he says the latter, tell her/him that the doctor has advised you that this weight loss is important for your present and future health, and that the doctor will tell you when to quit.

If the feeder tries to get you to eat, particularly something outrageously wrong, such as pie or cake, simply say, "My doctor told me that someone might try to get me off my diet, and he told me to say that I can't go off even a little bit." The usual response that a feeder makes to this is to say, "Oh, come on! A little bit of this won't hurt you." The thing that will shut up almost all feeders completely at this point is to say, "Well, my doctor said you might say that, too. He said if there were any question about whether I could eat it, then I am to get him on the phone and let you talk to him." This approach, along with a move toward the phone, will usually make the feeder leave you alone.

Remember one other thing as you progress on the

weight-loss program: *You owe no one any explanation or apology for going on a diet and helping your
health and appearance.*

One last thing about dealing with feeders. Know
who your friends really are. People who knowingly
try to get you off your diet are not your friends. They
are either malicious or ignorant, or both. In none of
these cases do you need to work with, socialize with,
or deal with this type of person. Put them behind you
if their attitude doesn't change and stay away from
them. You will find there are many other people in
the world who aren't like this, and among this better
group of people are those who can fill the gap left
by amputating the feeders from your group of friends.

Appendix 9

1. AVOID COUGH SYRUPS except for those listed here. All of the cough syrups on the market with the exception of Tussionex, Ryna-C, and Ryna-CX have loads of sugar. Especially avoid Nyquil and other nighttime cold medicines.

2. Avoid all throat lozenges and cough drops. Most of them have as much sugar as candy does. If you need something to soothe your throat, use either Chloraseptic spray or Cepastat liquid but never the Chloraseptic lozenges or the Cepastat lozenges. You may gargle with warm salt water but not with other commercial gargle preparations. The latter may be all right for freshening your breath but are out of place in the care of a sore throat.

3. You may take any product in tablet form that contains aspirin or Tylenol or a combination of these pain relievers. The only exception is a tablet that

contains caffeine. Never use caffeine-containing medicines because caffeine triggers hunger.

4. It is not really necessary to drink fruit juices when you have a cold or flu. You can get the same benefits from lots of water and sugar-free soda if you take vitamin C (ascorbic acid) tablets along with the calorie-free liquids. A good dosage of vitamin C is 500 to 1,000 milligrams taken four times daily. Any health food store or drug store will have this vitamin.

5. Never use whiskey, honey, vinegar, or a combination of these as a cold medicine. This will wreck your diet and not really help you. The same goes for the use of peppermint or other hard candies as a cough medicine; do not use them.

6. If you require medical treatment, show this book to your doctor with the names of the products mentioned in (7) below. The only antibiotic that is not compatible with the mineral and vitamin supplements is tetracycline and its derivatives. The calcium in the mineral formula tends to bind up the tetracycline and neither one of them is absorbed in the intestinal tract. If you must use tetracycline, omit the calcium tablet and magneisum until you are no longer taking the antibiotic, then resume them.

7. For cold and flu symptoms you may use several prescription tablets or capsules, including Tussend tablets (not the syrup), Unproco capsules, and Hycodan tablets. You may use Contac, Dristan, and Dimacol, all over-the-counter preparations, if desired. Use as directed or see your doctor.

8. You may use any over-the-counter antihistamine-decongestant tablet you desire, as long as it contains

no caffeine. You may also use any prescription medicine of the same category if it is in capsule or tablet form, but use no liquids.

9. The main thing to do when you have a cold is to rest your body and avoid stress to your system. There is no reason to go off your diet during this time, and eating to build up your strength will only make you gain weight. Avoid soups, broths, and other foods traditionally given to sick people. You might try herb teas with a little bit of fructose added to the hot liquid. It provides a pick-me-up and is delicious.

Appendix 10

AN OPEN LETTER TO
THE SPOUSE (OR PARENT
OR FRIEND) OF MY PATIENTS

YOU MAY THINK this is rather an unconventional thing to do, appealing to someone close to a dieter for help, but certain things need to be said to you or all of the dieter's efforts will be for naught, and the dieter will fail. For this reason, please carefully read everything that follows. All the things mentioned below do not apply in every case, but they are used as an example of things that could go wrong.

It is obvious that no one holds an overweight person down and makes him eat. In 99 percent of the cases, the person who is overweight is that way because he eats more food than he burns. What is not so obvious is the effect that the environment has on the overweight individual. Numerous scientific experiments have pointed out time and time again that the surroundings and external influences on a fat person have more to do with his problem eating behavior than the internal cues of hunger can ever have.

A large majority of overweight persons never experience a true feeling of hunger or of satiety (lack of hunger) as an individual of normal weight does. These experiments have shown that cues such as elapsed time from the most recent meals, smell, sight of food, activities usually associated with food (watching TV and eating), being in a certain location, and emotional upset will trigger massive food intake. These cues can make even the most compliant dieter vulnerable.

You may be asking yourself, "What does all this have to do with me? It isn't my problem. He or she should be able to diet by will power! Why involve me at all? If he can't do well, it is his weakness."

Nothing could be further from the truth. You are important, in fact more important than most of the people in the dieter's life, or you would not be reading this letter. If you are truly interested in helping the dieter, please take what is said here on faith for a while and see for yourself whether or not it is true. It may mean changing your own life-style a bit, but the results will be worthwhile.

To begin with, please never criticize the dieter for not dieting or for his or her eating habits. Ridicule, teasing, taunting, or other verbal abuse does not stop an undesirable behavior. It most likely will only make the overweight person want to eat more. You may have to bite your tongue to do so, but only comment on desirable behavior. If the patient is not breaking his or her diet, then comment on how good he or she is. If a lapse does occur, and this will happen, the less said the better. In the long run, positive reinforcement techniques work better for compliance to a diet. To repeat, even if you see something done wrong, please say nothing.

Since visual or olfactory cues are important in producing undesirable eating behavior, the dieter needs to fat-proof his dwelling. This means the cleaning out of all junk food that might tempt him. For the rest of your family, it may mean going out to get ice cream and not eating it or something equally tempting in front of the dieter. To eat such goodies in front of a dieter is the height of cruelty.

Many families are used to eating together, but the dieter may decide not to eat with you if he or she is bothered by sitting and watching others eat. He or she may simply take his or her meals and then get up right after finishing, even if others have not yet stopped eating. Many dieters are pickers, and if such a person remains at the table, he/she will find something to nibble on. Please be understanding, and at a later date when dieting efforts have been successful, the normal table behavior will be resumed.

A dieter may have to stay away from problem places, such as pizza parlors, taco stands, spaghetti houses, hamburger stands, take-out chicken˙stores, doughnut stores, and other equally tempting dens of obesity for dieters. Please don't bring this type of food home and tempt the dieter. The result is usually disastrous and is equivalent to tempting an alcoholic to go into a bar or bringing him a bottle of whiskey. No one in his right mind would do that to an alcoholic, but lots of people will try to "feed" a dieter.

What this message boils down to is that the dieter

is weak and does have some bad habits, but he is worth any and all efforts to help save him from the life-shortening effects of obesity. You and others may be incovenienced a little, but surely you can tolerate these minor annoyances for a while.

About one out of every hundred dieters is faced with overt or covert sadism or mental illness on the part of his or her spouse or a relative.

A certain type of person seems to feed on the misery of others, particularly of those who are fat. The archetype is the husband who keeps his wife fat, usually because of insecurity or other related reasons. He feels secure because she is so obese that no one else will have her. When his wife tries to lose weight, such a man becomes anxious and tries to get her to go off the diet by tempting her, annoying her, or by otherwise sabotaging her efforts. As she gets close to her weight goal, he becomes more and more anxious and will resort to physical abuse, verbal assaults, and as a last desperate effort may cut off her funds so she cannot continue her weight program. In such cases the majority succumb to the will of the "feeder" partner and stop dieting. For those who stick it out and continue the diet, there is divorce, usally coming on the heels of an increasing amount of abuse.

Not all victims are wives. Many are husbands of insecure wives or children of insecure parents. There is the case of a massively obese man whose wife constantly nagged him to eat, even while his doctor was present. She was jealous of him, and efforts to get him down to a safe weight were met with tirades and abuse that only ended when he stopped dieting. The woman now has what she wants, a husband so fat and unattractive that no one else would want him.

In summary, you and others who have close contact with the dieter have more influence on him or her than you will ever realize. Without your total assistance and support, the dieter will more than likely fail. The attitude that "food is love" is widespread. The idea that giving food is showing love and refusing food is rejecting love is still too strong for the comfort of most dieters. You can, however, show love in nonfood-related ways—for example, giving a bouquet of flowers on birthdays, Valentine's Day, and other holidays rather than a box of chocolates.

Bibliography

THIS BIBLIOGRAPHY is divided into two parts. The first part is an annotated list of books on dieting, exercise, and eating habits; the second part consists of a list of scientific literature that contains additional informa-iton on the fructose diet.

References

Brennan, R. O., M.D., with Mulligan, William C. *Nutri-genetics: New Concepts For Relieving Hypoglycemia.* New York: M. Evans and Co., Inc., 1976.
Good discussion of the symptoms and mechanisms of hypoglycemia.

Cooper, Kenneth H., M.D. *Aerobics,* New York: M. Evans and Co., Inc., 1968; *The New Aerobics.* New York: M. Evans and Co., Inc., 1970; and with Mildred Cooper, *Aerobics for Women,* New York: M. Evans and Co., Inc., 1972.
These are definitive information books on preparing your-self to be physically fit.

Crook, William G., M.D. *Are You Bothered by Hypoglycemia?* P.O. Box 3494, Jackson, Tenn., 38301. 1977. Booklet, *Professional Books Co.*

A simple, effective patient-instruction manual. Uses cartoons and diagrams to teach about hypoglycemia.

Ferguson, James M., M.D. *Habits, Not Diets.* Palo Alto, Calif.: Bull Publishing Company, 1976.

This is a manual that I use every day in my office. It is a classic of simplicity and of effective use of the programmed-instruction format.

Fredericks, Carlton, Ph.D. *Low Blood Sugar and You.* New York: Grosset and Dunlap, 1976.

One of the first books on hypoglycemia. Slightly outdated now and some of the reasoning is a little hard to accept, but still worth reading.

Jordan, Henry A., M.D., et al. *Eating Is Okay.* New York: Rawson Associates, 1977.

Good discussion of behavior modification.

Kraus, Barbara. *The Barbara Kraus 1978 Calorie Guide to Brand Names and Basic Foods.* New York: Signet, 1978.

Other books by Kraus offer information about food values.

Lappé, Frances Moore. *Diet for a Small Planet.* New York: Ballantine Books, 1975.

One of the best books in existence on vegetarian diets.

Lindner, Peter G., M.D. *Mind over Platter.* N. Hollywood, Calif.: Wilshire Book Company, 1963.

Dr. Lindner has also written several other publications for the use of physicians. Physicians wishing a complete list of his books should write him in care of the American Society for Bariatric Physicians in Englewood, Colorado (5200 South Quebec, Suite 300, Englewood, Colorado 80111). He is the most prolific writer of all the bariatricians in this country and has produced some of the best publications.

Palm, J. Daniel, Ph.D. *Diet Away Your Stress, Tension and Anxiety.* New York: Doubleday, 1976.

An excellent discussion of fructose and its effects.

Solomon, Neil, M.D. *Doctor Solomon's Easy, No-Risk Diet.*
New York: Coward, McCann and Geoghegan, 1974.
Interesting ideas, good calorie charts, and very orthodox
diet. Could work for some patients, but ignores the glucose-
insulin trap. Written by an excellent clinician and teacher.

Stuart, Richard B., and Davis, Barbara. *Slim Chance in a
Fat World.* Champaign, Ill.: Research Press, 1972.
One of the pioneer works in behavior modification, well
worth reading, but hard to find in bookstores.

Tyson, Richard, M.D., and Haims, Leonard, M.D. *How to
Triple Your Energy.* Chicago: Playboy Press, 1977.
A good discussion of Vitamins, energy metabolism, exercise, and the pitfalls of our modern life-style as it relates to
dieting. Dr. Haimes was a pioneer in bariatrics.

Scientific Literature on Fructose

Acta Medical Scandinavic, Supplement 542, 1972.
Has several thousand references. A very good primer on
fructose.

Advances in Carbohydrate Chemistry and Biochemistry, Vol-
ume 34, 1977, Academic Press, New York, pp. 286–343.
Over 400 references.
A must if you plan to use a lot of fructose in your practice.
American Journal of Clinical Nutrition

Journal of Biological Chemistry 252 (1977): 8,519–23.

Journal of Nutrition 93 (1967): 65–7.

Medical World News (August 7, 1978): 17–18.

Postgraduate Medical Journal 47 (1971): 654–9.

Proceedings of the Nutrition Society 35 (1977): 69A–70A.

*Proceedings of the Society of Experimental Biology and Medi-
cine* 94 (1957): 108–110.

Yale Journal of Biological Medicine 29 (1956/57): 335.

Index

Abdominal gas, 109
Alcohol, 45, 59, 94, 159-160
Amphetamines, 167
Antacids, 109
Antibiotics, 198
Artificial sweeteners, 44, 129
Asher, Wilmer, 79
Assertiveness, 85-88
Atkins diet, 157

Bad breath, 106
Basal needs, 30, 176-177
Basic Fructose Diet, 24, 38, 60-70
    fructose, 61
    protein, 61-64
    salads, 65
Beans, 45, 134
Behavior modification, 13
Beverages, 43-44, 58, 94, 182
Blood fat, 32

Blood pressure, 33
Blood sugar, 19-20
    See also Hypoglycemia
Bread, 45, 122, 128, 134
Butterworth Omelet, 185

Caffeine, 44, 58, 59, 139-140, 198
    side effects, 149
Calcium, 77
Caloric deficit, 151
Caloric needs, 30, 144, 167, 176-177
Candy, 45
Cannoli, 78, 123, 179
Carbohydrates, 17, 116-117, 154-155, 162-163
    low carbohydrate diets, 11, 24, 34-35, 148
Cereal, 45, 122, 134
Cheese, 76, 137, 138, 140

Cheesecake, 78, 123, 180, 182
Chicken Liver Omelet, 186
Cholesterol, 33
Cider vinegar, 158
Coffee, 44, 58, 149-150
Coffee break, 90
Cola, 149-150
    See also Sodas
Cold capsules, 198
Cold intolerance, 108
Colds, 111-112, 197-199
Constipation, 109
Cooking methods, 45, 47, 75
Cooper's Cannoli, 78, 123, 179
Cooper's Cheesecake, 78, 123, 180
Corn, 46, 134-135
Cottage cheese, 76, 122, 137, 138, 140
Cough syrups, 111, 197

Dependable Diet, 24, 39, 74-78
    cheese, 76
    eggs, 76
    fructose, 75
    meat, 75
    protein, 75-76
    salads, 76
    vegetables, 77
Desserts, 77-78, 123, 164, 179-182
Diabetics, 16, 22, 152, 171, 172
Diarrhea, 42, 110-111
Diary, 89, 103-104

Diet For A Small Planet, 142
Diet "monitor," 103
Diuretics, 66, 167
Dizziness, 108
Dr. Palm's Never Fail Fructose Fudge, 181
Dr. Palm's Swedish Cheesecake, 182
Doctors, 25, 67
Dry skin, 108

Eating habits, 89-92
Eggs, 59, 76, 140
Energy, 32, 34-35, 107
Epinephrine, 20, 21, 173
Estrogen, 168
Exercise, 30, 38, 127-128, 147-148, 153-154, 168-169
Exercise machines, 161

Faludi, Georgina, 16
Fats, 43, 136, 163
"Feeders," 99-100, 193-196
Ferguson, James M., 115
Fish, 64, 75, 139
Flank Steak, 186-187
Flounder-Fromage Fillet, 183
Flu, 111-112, 197-199
Fluid loss, 29
Fluids. See Beverages
Folic acid, 67
Fourteen Day Priming Diet, 38, 46-60
French lemonade, 58, 187
Fructose, 10, 148, 151-153, 156

Basic Fructose Diet, 61
  calories, 129
  controls hunger, 21, 28
  cost, 166
  and craving for sweets, 21
  Dependable Diet, 75
  and energy, 32, 34-35, 107
  in Europe, 152
  forms, 40-41, 59-60
  and insulin, 12, 32, 152,
    156-157
  Meals-and-Munch Diet, 72
  tolerance, 41-42
  Transition Diet, 120
  uses, 40-41
  Vegetarian Fructose Diet,
    78
Fruit, 129
  Permanent Diet, 132-133
  Transition Diet, 121-122
Fruit juices, 112, 122, 159,
    198
Fudge, 181

GTT, 16, 170
Galactose, 137, 155
Gas, abdominal, 109
Glandular malfunction, 186
Glucagon, 20, 21
Glucose, 34, 129, 137, 155-
    156
  levels, 174-175
  tolerance, 9-10, 16, 170
Glucose-Insulin Trap, 16-21,
    116, 152, 156-157, 170-
    171

Glucose-tolerance test, 16,
    170
Grapefruit juice, 158-159
Greece, obesity in, 147

Habits, Not Diet, 115
Hair growth, 110
Halitosis. See Bad breath
Headaches, 107
Herbs, 43
Heredity, 162
Hunger
  controlled, 21, 28
Hyperinsulinism, 18
Hypoglycemia, 16-17, 18, 19,
    34, 35, 153, 157, 171,
    172-173

Influenza. See Flu
Insomnia, 107-108
Insulin, 12, 32, 152
  See also Glucose-Insulin
    Trap
Italy, obesity in, 187

Ketosis, 28, 66, 106-107
Kool-Aid-like Beverage, 182

Lactose, 137, 155
Lappé, Frances Moore, 142
Laxatives, 109
Leftovers, 91
Lemonade, 42-43, 58, 187
Linoleic acid, 65

Liquids. *See* Beverages
Liver
    and glucose, 34-35
Loma Linda Foods, 81
Low blood sugar. *See* Hypo-
    glycemia

Maintenance program, 16,
    23-24
Maltose, 156
Meals-and-Munch Diet, 24,
    39, 70-74, 120
    fructose, 72
    salads, 72-73
    vegetables, 73-74
Measurements, 126-127
Meat, 64, 75, 139, 141, 142-
    143
Meditation, 98
Menstrual irregularities, 109
Mental attitude, 95-96
Milk, 46, 122, 137, 138
Milkshake Diet, 39-40, 178
Mouthwashes, 106

Nausea, 107
NIOFast diet, 178
Nuts, 137

Omelets, 185, 186
Orange Delight Salad Dress-
    ing, 183
Osmotic diarrhea, 110-111

Paddington Quiche, 187

Palm, J. Daniel, 12, 152
Parrot technique, 86-87, 100
Parties, 93-94, 195
Pasta, 46, 135
Peanut butter, 141
Permanent Diet, 124-144
    fruit, 132-133
    protein, 126
    vegetables, 131
Postural hypotension, 108
Potassium, 45, 48, 49, 58-59,
    66-67, 77
Potatoes, 46, 122, 135
Poultry, 64, 75
Pregnant women, 22, 109-
    110
Prepared foods, 142, 161-162
Processed food. *See* Prepared
    foods
Protein, 30-31, 70, 75, 105,
    139-141, 162-163
    Basic Fructose Diet, 61-64
    Dependable Diet, 75-76
    high protein diet, 24, 34-
        35, 148
    loss, 31, 33
    Permanent Diet, 126
    shares, 47, 61-64, 142-143
    sources, 31, 64
    Transition Diet, 123
    vegetable, 78-79

Quiche, 187

*Rapid Weight Reduction
    (RWR) Program, The,*
    79

Relaxation, 97-98
Restaurants, 165-166
Rice, 46, 135

Saccharin, 44, 129
Safflower oil, 65
Salad dressings, 65-66, 73, 76, 137, 183-184
Salads, 57, 65, 72-73, 76, 79, 185
Salmon Crispies, 188
Salt, 68, 123-124
Sauces, 58, 142
Scallops, 184
Sea Food Dip, 185
Seasoning, 43, 58, 123, 141
Self-image, 95-96
Shellfish, 64, 75, 139
Shopping, 92-93
Side effects, 105-112
Skin, dry, 108
Socioeconomic class and obesity, 147
Sodas, 44, 58, 149-150, 189
Soft drinks. See Sodas
Sorbitol, 111, 129
Sour Cream Pudding, 181
Spices, 43
Spring Garden Salad, 185
Stress, 12, 19, 23, 34, 96-101, 115, 153, 163-164
Stuffed Flank Steak, 186-187
Stuffed Green Pepper, 185-186
Sucrose, 155
Sugar, 59, 128
    consumption, 161

hidden, 105
    types, 155
Sugar-free sodas, 44, 58
Supplements. See Potassium; Vitamin supplements
Suppliers, 190-192
Sweat suits, 160
Sweeteners, artificial, 44, 129

Tea, 58, 150
Testosterone, 168
Tetracycline, 198
Transition Diet, 114-124
    fructose, 120
    fruit, 121-122
    protein, 123
    vegetable, 120-121
Triglycerides, 32, 33, 130
Tuna Crispies, 188

Vegetables, 78-79, 162-163
    Dependable Diet, 77
    Meals-and-Munch Diet, 73-74
    Permanent Diet, 131
    Transition Diet, 120-121
Vegetarian Fructose Diet, 24, 39, 78-82, 165
    fructose, 78
    salads, 79
Vegetarians, 142
Vinaigrette Salad Dressing, 183-184
Vinegar and Oil Salad Dressing, 184

Vitamins, 45, 58, 67-68, 74,
    77, 79-80, 120
  Vitamin C, 112, 198

Walking, 127, 168-169
Water, 44, 58, 70, 106, 157-
    158

Water loss, 29
Weigh-ins, 125-126
Weight loss, 29-31
Worthington Foods, 82

Yogurt, 46, 122, 138, 181